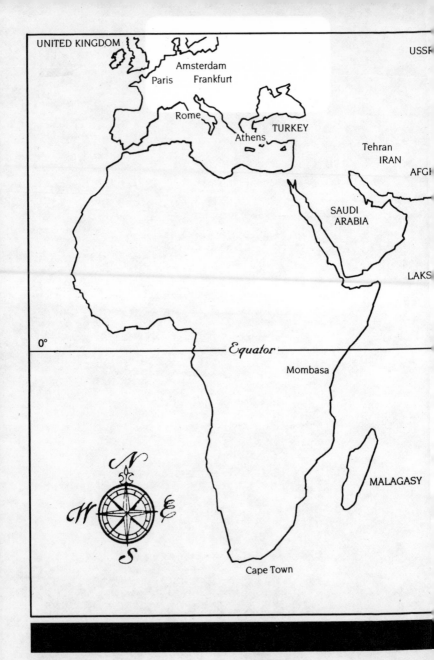

Indian Ocean

maldives

Stuart Bevan

Other People publications

Published by Other People, Australia.

Typeset by J. & M. Cruickshanks Phototypesetting, Australia.
Printed by South China Printing Company, Hong Kong.
Cartography by Grassroot Graphics, Australia.

First edition 1982
Second edition 1985

National Library of Australia
Cataloguing-in-Publication entry:

Bevan, Stuart.
    Maldives.

    Bibliography.
    Includes index.
    ISBN 0 9590626 0 2.
    1. Maldives — Description and travel — Guide-books.
    I. Title.

915.49'504

Contents

Part Four

Part Five

Introduction

More and more travellers are in search of new unspoilt destinations. Their most recent discovery is a nation of islands looping the equator, at the centre of the Indian Ocean.

It's a natural paradise, a world of intensely simple beauty, a place that will captivate the mind and rest the human spirit. Travel brochures will tell you it's "the best kept secret in the world". Which really means: "See it soon!".

Some people have been there for a visit and stayed a lifetime, others have left within a day. The Maldives is that sort of place — fascinating for some, frustrating for others.

These islands are no place for the old, the frail and fragile, the pampered Hilton Hotel people, the fastidious, the gourmet, the night-clubber — and so on. They are for those who are adventurous and young-at-heart, those exhilarated by tropical surroundings and unfussed by minor discomforts. Indeed they are for people who care to realise their Robinson Crusoe fantasies.

The author of this book, Stuart Bevan, was driven by a hunger to learn as much as he could from the Maldivian people and their way of life. During his five-year sojourn, he accumulated the experience and information recalled in the following pages. He hopes that this book will help you not only to see, but to know the Maldives.

Virginia Greig was equally drawn to the unique island simplicity and lent her aesthetic and culinary talents to this book, many of them learnt while stoking the stove on a far-flung desert island.

Onny Martin worked for some years at the Maldives' Earth Station and in his spare time recorded his account of the islands — in photographs. Despite being arrested for climbing the Earth Station tower and supposedly spying on the local jail, his camera and photographs still live, some in this book.

Jo Cormack worked as a voluntary school teacher and before long there were lots of little pig-tailed Maldivian Cormackites gaily conversing around Male in their broad, strong Lancashire accents. During her stay she uncovered an amazing stream of data from an equally amazing array of sources, all of which proved helpful in some way.

Ibrahim Hameed was educated at a university in New Zealand and proferred a surface study of the Maldivian language which proved invaluable when preparing this book.

Hassan Maniku, who acts as Director for the Maldives Department of Information and enjoys a wide local reputation as academic and author, offered a wealth of informative literature.

And John Kingsmill offered patient encouragement and his thoughts on writing style.

Hasan Ramiz, an Italian Swiss-born traveller, married a woman from the southern atolls, fathered children and wishes little more than "a poor but human and relaxing life". His keen insight into many aspects of local life, his artistic flair and, above all else, his sense of humour — which included the thought provoking question: *foi liani ki kurang?* (why are you writing this book?) — was an endless source of encouragement.

Others who have contributed to *Maldives* in one or many ways are sincerely thanked under a single title — other people.

The islands

. . . *the flower of the Indies*

Marco Polo

. . . *one of the wonders of the world*

Ibn Battuta

. . . *they look like an orchard*

Joao de Barros

Few countries have a landscape as remarkable as that of the Maldives, pronounced morl-dives (as in "gives"). Ancient travellers once knew it as *Maladiv*, meaning a garland of islands, and now the inhabitants call it *Divehi Rajje* — the Island Kingdom.

It is an archipelago of 1300 islands — give or take a few, say the locals who are used to "discovering" the odd island — spanning the equator about 650kms southwest of Sri Lanka (formerly known as Ceylon). On a map the islands resemble a cartographer's error, a spray of ink, but in reality they stretch across a chain-like formation extending 764kms from north to south and 130kms at the widest point. The islands are dispersed over twenty-six atolls (derived from the local term *atolu*), or ring-like coral formations each enclosing a deep blue lagoon and one or more islands formed from coral debris. As the water becomes shallower on approach to the island or sandbank, the deep blue of the sea is mottled with bright turquoise.

It is still a matter of much debate as to when and how these atolls were formed, but in 1842, Charles Darwin proferred the first acceptable theory. He suggested that atolls were created when a volcanic land mass subsided slowly into the ocean, while coral built up and out around the plateaux. However, in a postscript, Darwin noted that the Maldives were somehow different, quite unlike the atolls he had examined in the Pacific and Atlantic Oceans.

But not until 1962 were the peculiarities of the Maldivian atolls studied.

Hans Hass, an eminent German scientist, made a diving expedition through the archipelago and concluded that "the inner structure of certain coral reefs is not compact but porous and unstable, hence extended reef platforms invariably sag in the centre. And the depth of the lagoons may be explained by crystallisation and the perishing of the coral substance, reinforced by the cumulative effect of the tides".

In other words, changing sea levels, tectonic activity and an amazing coral evolutionary process have created, over millenia, a series of reefs along the peaks of the vast submerged mountain range which extends through the centre of the Indian Ocean. And by raising the reef a fraction of a centimetre each year the coral has finally pierced the surface of the ocean, where it began to form a platform.

According to Hass, the centre of the platform eventually subsides due to the perishing of the coral substance (the live coral suffocates when food and oxygen are scarce) and the massaging effect of the tides. Around the rim of the atoll, however, where the coral has built hardest and highest, sand and debris accumulate, vegetation takes hold and islands begin to form.

Throughout the Maldives the islands are never any bigger than a few square kilometres nor higher than a few metres above sea level. In fact, the largest is only 6kms long, and the highest is less than three metres above sea level. But the atolls — or rings of islands if you will — often extend some 30 or 40kms from north to south and 20kms at the widest point.

Ancient mariners often likened the Maldives to a wall in the middle of the sea, where entry and exit could be made only via a few narrow channels. Therefore, it is hardly surprising that this stretch of the Indian Ocean is renowned as a place of shipwrecks, and it is regarded as foolhardy to navigate the archipelago without an experienced local *daturu miha* (traveller) close at hand.

The weather

In a nation more sea than land, the weather must obviously play a significant role in day-to-day life. Since earliest times the Maldivian people, living in a "country" where more than 99% of the total territory is sea, have lived according to a *nakai* calendar — a series of thirteen and fourteen day intervals, each with a predictable pattern of weather.

Every year brings two monsoons called *iruva* (northeast) and *hulungu* (southwest). To the layman it simply means hot and dry, or hot and wet. But to the Maldivian it means a series of *nakai* which will basically determine lifestyles for the next six months. Even today this calendar is used to determine the best times to fish, or travel, or cultivate crops. And some people may even use it before planning a marriage or building a house.

The calendar goes something like this:

Iruva

Dec 10-22		
	dry, some showers	*Mula nakai*
Dec 23-Jan 5		
	dry, good fishing	*Furuhala*
Jan 6-18		
	dry, fishing fair, plant some millets	*Uturuhala*
Jan 19-31		
	dry, bonito biting	*Huvan*
Feb 1-13		
	dry, fishing season	*Dinasha*
Feb 14-26		
	dry, fishing good	*Hiyaviha*
Feb 27-Mar 11		
	sunshowers, great fishing, clean and burn the land	*Furaboduruva*
Mar 12-25		
	sunshowers, great fishing, prepare the soil	*Fasaboduruva*
Mar 26-Apr 7		
	dry, fishing fair	*Reva*

Hulungu

Apr 8-21		
	hot and dry, poor fishing, plant millets and trees	*Assida*
Apr 22-May 5		
	dry, strong winds, heavy seas, continue planting	*Burunu*
May 6-19		
	sometimes wet, sometimes dry	*Keti*
May 20-Jun 2		
	storms	*Rornu*

Date	Description	Name
Jun 3-16	thunderstorms, travelling bad	*Miyaheli*
Jun 17-30	light showers, schools of fish	*Ada*
Jul 1-14	wet or dry, travelling difficult	*Funors*
Jul 15-28	dry and overcast, good fishing	*Fus*
Jul 29-Aug 10	sunny days, fishing fair	*Ahuliha*
Aug 11-23	light rain	*Maa*
Aug 24-Sep 6	sunshowers	*Fura*
Sep 7-20	some rain, bad fishing	*Utura*
Sep 21-Oct 3	sunshowers, schools of fish	*Ata*
Oct 4-17	sunshowers and strong winds, fishing fair	*Hita*
Oct 18-30	storms	*Hey*
Nov 1-13	storms or sunshine, fishing bad	*Viha*
Nov 14-26	dry and sunny, fishing season in the north	*Nora*
Nov 27-Dec 9	dry and cloudy, fishing season in the south	*Dosha*

In tourist jargon the monsoons are simply called "high" and "low". From November until April, groups of tourists flock to the islands to enjoy the endless blue skies and day-long sunshine. And from May until October, when the weather is a mixed bag of sunshine, showers and storms, tourist prices are generally slashed to entice the visitor in spite of the weather.

Year-round the temperature rarely falls below 25°C, more often than not hovering around 30°C, and the average annual rainfall is only 168mm (about seven inches) — although in the south, down towards the equator, the rainfall is more variable.

Vegetation and fauna

On most islands, the natural vegetation is, on a small scale, much like that of lowland Sri Lanka: tropical rainforest with banyan, bamboo, screwpine, vines, herbs and mangroves. And of course the ubiquitous coconut palm.

Animal life is restricted to a few migrating frigate birds, sleek grey herons, sparrows, and bats suckling on the sweet honey of the coconut palms. And where there are villages there are rats, cats and chickens, and in some places a few goats and a solitary cow.

Not surprisingly, the fauna in the Maldives is in greatest profusion around the coral reefs. It is said that more than seven hundred species of fish live in the Indian Ocean and many diving enthusiasts claim to have seen most of them around the Maldive islands. Long-time divers say that nowhere else in the world can compare with the spectacular underwater scenery of the Maldives, where even the novice can don a mask and snorkel and be sure to see a swarm of multi-coloured reef fish. And the adventurous divers who explore the deep sea cays and caverns are quite likely to find a school of over-fed "friendly" sharks, a huge manta ray or a moray eel.

And of course everywhere there are tuna, skipjack and bonito — the lifeblood of the islands.

Coral

The gardens of coral that decorate these shallow, tropical waters are not, as they appear, plants. In fact, these incredible creatures are built up by aggregations of tiny tentacled animals, polyps, which battle through life against a host of enemies — crustaceans, protozoans, reef fish, star fish and man.

Basically these amazing animals need only three things to survive: food, oxygen and warmth. They feed happily on plankton, receive oxygen (up to fifty metres below the ocean's surface) from the sun, and thrive in clear, salty water where the temperature is between 20° and 30° centigrade.

And, like most other animals, these polyps secrete and have sex, and herein lies the secret of the reef. After extracting the soluble calcium ions from the surrounding sea water they excrete a cup-like limestone skeleton — in much the same way as an oyster secretes its protective shell — and come out to feed, usually at night when the plankton is most plentiful. It is this minuscule limestone cup, produced by billions of polyps, that accounts for the rock-like texture of the coral reef.

And it is the fascinating process by which the polyps reproduce that explains the variety of shapes, sizes and colours along the reef. As the new moon arrives during the winter months and the full moon during the summer months, the polyps engage in sexual and asexual encounters, producing planula, or offspring, by the multiple billions, and though many of them die as they are born, enough survive to perpetuate the species — and the reef.

The survivors are washed to and fro by the ocean currents, then finally attach themselves to a solid foundation — a submerged volcano or a coastline — and secrete, reproduce and eventually form a colony of polyps, which, over a millenium, grows larger and more complex, until a thin ribbon of reef runs parallel to the foundation.

The reef — or the colony of polyps if you will — survives best on the seaward side. Elsewhere, particularly between the reef and the shore, the colonies gradually die off due to lack of food, or under attack by their lifelong enemies. For example a parrot fish — and there are multitudes of them in the Maldives — can easily chew coral with its massive beaklike jaw, and pass limestone as beach sand in prodigious quantities. Indeed researchers say that a single medium-sized parrot fish will pass about one ton of sand in a year, so it's little wonder that most islands are surrounded by sandy shallows and shorelines.

Ironically, however, it is the inhabitants who live on these islands — people whose lives depend on the protection afforded by the reef — who are the polyp's number one enemy. The renowned deep-sea explorer, Jacques Cousteau, was alarmed when he discovered what the Maldivian people were doing to their coral reefs. In the *Ocean World of Jacques Cousteau* he writes:

> Traditionally the islanders built their houses of thatch (but) as the modern world began to catch up with the islands, large buildings and roads had to be built and the only construction material available was that from the coral reef. Now the Maldivians harvest the coral year round, using large chunks of it as building blocks. By destroying the fringing coral reefs, the Maldive people are unknowingly dooming their islands, for without a protective ring to shield the atolls from the pounding trade-wind waves, the islands must themselves disappear.

So for those who care to conserve what has taken billions of years to create, think again if you're tempted to take home a piece of the reef, however small, as a souvenir.

History

Information concerning the origins of the Maldivian people — or the *Divehin* (islanders) as they prefer to be called — is a curious mixture of myth and fact, as is the way with history. According to some observers, the islands were first discovered by travellers who explored the oceans of the world in reed ships. Thor Heyerdahl, renowned *Kon Tiki* explorer, recently visited the southern atolls and discovered a set of coral slabs bearing images and scripts which, he says, closely resemble those of the ancient Indus Valley civilsation that thrived in modern-day Pakistan between 2500 and 1500BC.

But according to the most popular folklore, the Maldives was first colonised by an Indo-Aryan race between the fourth and fifth centuries BC. In a translation by H.C.P. Bell, an archaeologist formerly with the Ceylon Civil Service, the legend goes something like this:

> Once upon a time, when the Maldives were still sparsely inhabited, a Prince of royal birth named Koimala Kalo, who had married the King of Ceylon's daughter, made a voyage with her in two vessels from Serendib Island. Reaching the Maldives, they were becalmed and rested awhile at Rasgetimu Island, in North Malosmadulu Atoll.
>
> The Maldive islanders learning that the two visitors were of Royal Ceylonese descent, invited them to remain, then ultimately proclaimed Koimala their King at Rasgetimu, the original King's Island.
>
> Subsequently, Koimala and his spouse migrated thence to Male about AH500 (beginning of the twelfth century AD) and settled there with the consent of the aborigines of Giraavaru Island, then the most important community of Male Atoll.
>
> To Koimala and his Queen was born a male child who was called Kalaminja. He reigned as a Buddhist for twelve years and was then converted to Islam, ruling for thirteen years more before finally departing for Mecca.
>
> This ruler's daughter married the Chief Minister and reigned as nominal Sultana. She gave birth to a son also called Kalaminja, who in turn married a lady of the country.
>
> From them the subsequent rulers of the Maldives were descended.

19

Other sources and archaeological finds suggest that the Koimala Kalo legend, for whatever it is worth, is obviously post-dated by many centuries.

And whatever truth lies behind this legend, one thing is certain — the early day settlers came via Sri Lanka and practised some ancient Buddhist customs. Testimony to this is the modern-day language called *Divehi*, which is akin to Elu, an ancient form of Sinhala (the Sri Lankan language), and the ancient Maldivian scripts, *Evala Akuru* (letters written on copper plates) and *Dives Akuru* (letters seen on some of the age-old tombstones and on old documents and boards which are held in the National Museum). The scripts bear strongest resemblance to a medieval Sinhala alphabet, and the recently foregone *foi kakkan* festival — once celebrated by the Maldivians at a particular full moon, seemingly in celebration of the first time rice was brought to the islands — is said to be closely related to the Sri Lankan commemoration of the attainment of Nirvana by Gautama Buddha. And then there are the ancient relics which have been found on some of the islands — relics which closely resemble the monuments found in the ancient Buddhist capitals of Sri Lanka.

But reference to age-old navigational charts and travellers' tales suggests that the present-day population is descendant not only from an ancient Buddhist culture but also from a pot pourri of cultures — Arab travellers, Dravidians and Aryans from India and slaves from Africa were all, at one time or another, part of early Maldivian civilisations. Evidence of this can be found in the works of H.C.P. Bell, who visited the islands in 1888, 1920 and 1940. Among other things, he published a copy of the *Tarikh*, the major Maldivian chronicle, which offers a brief account of life and times in the Maldives between 1153 and 1821. This work is complemented by a short travelogue prepared by Ibn Battuta, who lived in the islands during the mid-fourteenth century, and by a more detailed volume published by Francois Pyrard, who spent five years in the capital after he was shipwrecked in 1602. And coupled with this is the nineteenth century memoir by Young and Christopher, two naval officers, who offer an insight into more recent customs and manners.

The aborigines

Not much is known about the aborigines who purportedly met Koimala and his wife nearly two thousand years ago. Indeed all that is known is gleaned from the small community of *Giraavaru* people, found in the outskirts of the capital. They claim they are descendent from a Tamil tribe, originally from southern India and once the most powerful people of the Maldives.

And although regarded nowadays as somewhat inferior to the "average" Maldivian, the *Giraavaru* still maintain their unique identity. The women, for example, wear their hair in a bun on the left side of the head while other women wear theirs on the right, and they alone wear a wide white embroidery around the neck of their dress. Sexual morality is high on their list of virtues, and in fact is one characteristic where they feel themselves far superior to the *Divehin*. They go so far as to consider it immoral for the woman to ever bare her body in front of a man, husband or otherwise, so petticoats have an appropriately embroidered hole.

As seems the way with aboriginal tribes in the history of mankind, the *Giraavaru* people, over the years, have been stripped of their land and given no encouragement for the advancement of their own culture. They are generally poorer than their Maldivian counterparts, hence the modern-day Maldivian tends to see them as "dirty and stupid". So the young *Giraavaru* today tries as soon as he can to enter the mainstream Maldivian life, intermarry and, inevitably, the *Giraavaru* culture is dying.

The Arabs

The most profound impact on the history-culture of the Maldives came from the ancient Arab travellers. As early as the ninth century AD, they had spread their influence and knowledge across the Asian mainland, and the Maldives — or *Dibajat* as it was known to them — was a popular entrepôt enroute to other ports of call. Here they could take on water and food (dried fish, coconuts and the like), buy a few local products and even enjoy a "temporary wife". Ibn Battuta once noted that it was the most agreeable society he had ever seen — and he had seen ninety-two countries. He remarked that "any newcomer could marry if he so desired, then on leaving he simply repudiated his wife". In those days, however, the greatest attraction was the small white mollusc, the cowrie shell, which clung to driftwood and lay on the island shores in abundance. It was the local currency and could be used to buy slaves from Africa and sacks of rice from India. The Arabs bought them by the boat load.

The first outstanding milestone in Arab-Maldivian relations occurred in 1153 — the year of the Islamic conversion. Legend has it that Abu al-Barakat, the most pious saint of the age, arrived in the Maldives and discovered a "colony of ignorant idolators". He set about converting the King to Islam by exorcising a *jinni* (spirit) which apparently arose from the sea each month to molest and murder a local virgin girl. And from then on the Maldives became wholly Islamic, receiving Arab visitors with much esteem, electing some as Sultans and others as *gazis* (judges).

The Ali Rajas and Portuguese

Until the turn of the fifteenth century trade between the Maldives and the mainland depended largely on the Moslem merchants on the southwest coast of India. They were known as the "Sea Kings", or the Ali Rajas of Cannanore. And so widespread was their influence that they also became affectionately, or otherwise, known as "Lords of the Maldive Islands"

During the early years of the sixteenth century, however, the islands were no longer the sacred realm of the Ali Rajas, for now the newly-arrived and more powerful Portuguese forces began demanding a share in all the lucrative Indian Ocean trade routes. Hence, following a successful coup d'etat and the reinstatement of Kalu Muhammed, "a tyrant, heartless deceitful ruler", the Portuguese were granted many liberties, such as permission to build a factory and a fort on the capital island. And fifty years later, in 1552, another Sultan, Hasan IX, invited the Portuguese to take complete control of the islands. It was a contract not without strings attached, for the bulk of the population fought vehemently before finally succumbing, in 1558, to the Portuguese "infidels", and for the next seventeen years "the sea grew red with Moslem blood" as the locals were forcibly instructed in Christian beliefs and customs.

The eventual downfall of the "infidels" came late one night, on December 17, 1573. Muhammed Thakurufanu, island chief of Utheemu, led a small band of followers, approached Male harbour and set about slaughtering the Portuguese soldiers. But only after several aborted attempts to regain control of the islands were the Portuguese persuaded to accept a treaty which provided full independence to the Maldives. They did insist, however, that they retain sole trading rights to and from the islands and demanded a royal pension for Hasan IX, the so-called "Christian King".

By the turn of the sixteenth century it became apparent that the Sultan need no longer provide the Portuguese with tributes and trade monopolies, for the Dutch had now established themselves as the major force in the Indian Ocean. A diplomatic relationship was soon created between the Sultan of the Maldives and the Governor of Sri Lanka, and in return for access to the cowrie treasury the Dutch Governor promised an annual supply of spices, arecanut and ammunition.

Nevertheless, there were others interested in the islands' offerings. Following the Sultan's attack on Minicoy, part of modern-day Lakshadweep (formerly Laccadives), an Indian territory, the Ali Rajas sent several retaliatory forces to the islands. In 1752 they succeeded in destroying the palace, kidnapping the Sultan and taking control of the government. But their victory was short-lived, for within a matter of months, they were ousted following a local uprising and the arrival of a small French fleet.

The British and Borahs

In 1796, the Dutch ceded Sri Lanka to the British and a regular trade route was quickly established between Colombo and Male. But due to the "somnolent, spendthrift Sultan", the islands were on the verge of total bankruptcy until the Borah merchants were invited, in 1860, to set up godowns and shops on the capital island. In no time at all, these astute Moslem merchants from India obtained an almost complete monopoly on the import and export trade and even began financing major government projects. The result was inevitable: Borahs would soon rule the Maldives.

Local businessmen, sensing the dangers, reacted by burning down the major godowns and shops, and the British Governor signed a treaty with the Sultan which guaranteed their full independence in return for Sovereign status.

In 1887, the Maldives became a British protectorate.

The 20th century

Twentieth century Maldives has been battered and shaped by time and nature, coups and constitutions, Sultans and Presidents. The following occurrences were among the most significant to take place during this century.

1900 The Sultanate was in debt to Carimjee Jaferjee and Co., the largest of the Borah merchants in the Maldives. Political factions emerged and the Sultan, Muhammed Imaduddin VI, was prompted to sack his Prime Minister, Ibrahim Didi.

1902 Imaduddin left for Egypt in search of a "stately wife" and a revolution brewed at home.

1903 The British sent an envoy to the Maldives to investigate rumours of "injustice, oppression, misanthropy and misrule" levelled at Imaduddin.

1904 The British Governor recognised Muhammed Shamsuddin III as the new Sultan, despite protestations from Imaduddin and friends.

1905 With the help of family and Indian pirates, Imaduddin made several futile attempts to regain control of the Sultanate.

Also in this year, the *Crusader* was wrecked on a reef and Lloyds of London questioned the age-old Maldivian salvage law, which claimed "that half the salvaged goods from any ship wrecked in the Maldives shall be the property of the government". The British Government's response was total non-interference. And as others have noted more recently, the law is much the same today.

1906 Shamsuddin opened the first post office, which provided a regular mail service to Colombo.

1917 A British sea-plane crashed in the central atolls, and a German warship lurked around the southern atolls.

1920 Shamsuddin was awarded the Most Distinguished Order of Saint Michael and Saint George by the British.

1922 An epidemic swept through the capital causing over three hundred deaths. It was known amongst travellers as "Maldive fever". It was, in fact, malaria.

1923 A storm devastated many islands and villages in the north of the archipelago.

1924 Imaduddin's son, 'Abd-Allah, was allowed a re-entry visa but he was soon deported when the Sultan's secret service unearthed his plot to overthrow the government.

1932 Shamsuddin was forced to accept a constitution that would limit his power — the first-ever written constitution in the Maldives.

1934 Shamsuddin was sacked for attempting to side-step the constitution and Sultan Nuruddin took the throne.

1939 The British constructed an airstrip at Kelaa and another at Gan, as a back-up for its defence of Singapore and India.

The constitution was discarded, being "unsuitable to local conditions".

1942 The second constitution was drawn up.

1943 Nuruddin was forced to abdicate, being "unsuitable to the constitution". Abdul Majeed Didi was elected Sultan No. 93, but he was old and retired to Colombo while Muhammed Amin Didi, the Prime Minister, assumed almost complete control of the government. Virtually overnight, he introduced a widespread modernisation program, which included a National Security Service and a government monopoly on the export of fish. And being a health fanatic he banned the smoking of tobacco.

1948 A Mutual Defence Pact was signed with the British.

1953 The Sultanate was abolished and Didi was elected President of the Republic of Maldives. But food shortages and the ban on smoking had incurred the wrath of thousands, and upon returning from an overseas holiday, Didi was attacked and arrested. He died in hospital on March 7.

The Republic was abolished, the constitution discarded.

1954 Muhammad Farid Didi, son of Abdul Majeed Didi, was elected Sultan.

1955 On January 9 another storm destroyed the villages in the north.

1956 An agreement was drafted with the British, providing a one-hundred-year lease of Gan for £2,000 a year. Although the agreement was not yet formalised, the British began developing an RAF staging post and employed hundreds of locals as labourers, store-keepers and kitchen hands.

1957 Ibrahim Nasir was elected Prime Minister. He revoked the '56 agreement on Gan and insisted that the lease be shortened, the rental increased and all local employees sacked.

1959 The inhabitants of the three southernmost atolls, protesting that the "Male government had reduced them to serfs", united and formed the United Suvadive Islands. Abdulla Afif Didi was elected President, a People's Council was formed, a trading corporation established and a bank founded. Their needs, wants and demands were then published in the international press.

1960 Rumours spread far and wide that somehow the British were behind "the situation in the Maldives", so to temper suspicions, Nasir's demands regarding the lease of Gan were formalised: a thirty-year lease for £100,000 a year — plus a grant of £750,000 for general development and a new fully-equipped hospital in Male. Nasir then asserted his supreme authority and invaded the southern atolls with armed launches, forcing Didi to flee to the Seychelles. The United Suvadive Islands was leaderless, and finally quashed.

1965 On July 26 the British relinquished all Protectorate status, thus the Maldives became fully independent and later joined the United Nations.

1968 The Sultan was encouraged to retire to Colombo with a royal pension, and on November 11 Ibrahim Nasir was elected President of the second Republic.

Few countries can lay claim to as much foreign influence as that experienced by the Maldives in the 1970s and early 1980s.

1972 The constitution was amended to give Nasir far-reaching powers and he made the most of his dictatorial authority by opening his own hotel and travel agency, government-financed. Nearly one thousand visitors arrived to stay at Viharafushi (modern-day Kurumba) and the idea to develop the country as a "tropical paradise" was thereby launched.

1974 Despite the immediate and obvious benefits derived from the ever-growing tourist traffic, most of the people still suffered from escalating food prices. On Thursday, June 24, a large crowd gathered to protest, but Nasir retaliated by ordering the police to open fire. The revolt became colloquially known as "little troubles Thursday" and represented the first popular uprising against Nasir's regime.

1975 Ahmed Zaki was elected to a second term as Prime Minister and rumours quickly spread that a no-confidence motion against Nasir was in the offing. But before any action could be taken Zaki and eleven other ministers were banished to faraway islands. The event became popularly known as "big troubles Thursday".

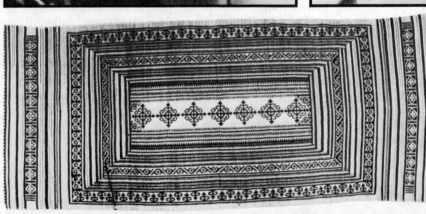

1978 Nasir retired, ostensibly for "health reasons", and departed, purportedly with the bulk of the national treasury, to live in Singapore. On November 11 Maumoon Abdul Gayoom, the first Maldivian ambassador to the United Nations, was elected President. In his first few days in office he denounced the former regime.

1979 A number of Nasir's cronies were banished to faraway islands, and extradition proceedings were initiated to have Nasir returned to stand trial for corruption, theft and murder.

1980 A coup against Gayoom's government was aborted. Two British mercenaries were arrested, tried and deported. A number of Nasir's relatives and affluent friends were arrested or banished, and another unsuccessful attempt was made to extradite Nasir.

1981-2 Gayoom began forming a new-style government, broadening international contacts and introducing innovative development programs. The first regional hospital was opened on Kulhudhuffushi, in the northernmost atoll, and another was planned for Hithadhoo, in the southernmost atoll. An indoor sports stadium was erected in Male, an international airport was opened on Hulhule, and the first domestic flight was operated to the southernmost atolls. The government also took control of the Japanese fish-canning factory in Laviyani atoll and collaborated with foreign investors to open garment factories on Gan.

Before the end of 1982 the Maldives had extended its diplomatic ties to more than fifty countries and its membership to twenty-two international organisations. A cultural treaty was signed with Libya and a trade agreement with Sri Lanka, support was officially proclaimed for the Palestinian cause, and the Maldives was made a special member of the Commonwealth of Nations.

1983 In August another feeble attempt was made to depose Gayoom, before he was elected, in November, to a second term as President.

1984 The frequency of chartered and scheduled flights to the Maldives was increased to accommodate the ever-increasing flow of tourists — from less than one thousand a year to seventy thousand in just twelve years.

The people

In times past, travellers saw Maldivians as:

poor looking creatures Jean Parmentier
honest and pious, sincere and strong-willed Ibn Battuta
quick and apprehensive, subtle and crafty Francois Pyrard
sober, honest and cheerful C. W. Rosset
constructive and ordered Dr Campbell
quiet, peaceable, hospitable and kind, but suspicious and distrustful of strangers Young & Christopher
dull, feeble and malicious Duarte Barbosa

With a total population of less than 150,000 the Maldives represents the smallest independent nation in Asia, and with an average per capita income less than $US200 a year, it is one of the poorest nations in the world. Yet, astonishingly, there are no beggars and the grinding poverty found in other parts of Asia is rarely seen on the islands. According to Bell the people "desire nothing so greatly as to be left by the outside world, as much as possible, alone and undisturbed in their sea-girt happy isolation".

The majority of these people live their lifetime on a tiny island, where interaction is limited to a few hundred fellow islanders. To this day the *don miha* (white man) may be regarded with fear and suspicion, so don't be surprised if you are met on a far-flung island by screeching children, women in flight, and a cold, pensive stare from the men. But human nature is paradoxical and the Maldivians can be all things at once. They can be as bold as they are shy, as knowledgeable as they are naive.

So to accept and be accepted by this small, closely-knit, rigidly structured, disciplined society demands a fundamental appreciation of the politics, beliefs and customs of its people.

The political system

Nearly four hundred years ago, Francois Pyrard wrote "the people live under a system of law and police". It is still much the same today, it's just "purer and more civilised", according to Bell.

Basically there are three levels of government forming the political infrastructure. At the bottom is the island administration. Every citizen is registered at one of the 202 inhabited islands and each family is given a small plot of land (about 15x30 metres) on the island on which they were born or have lived for twelve or more years. This, of course, discourages mass migration to other islands and serves to reinforce the very foundation of the political framework.

Each of the inhabited islands is ruled by a *kateeb* (chief) and one or more *kuda* (little) *kateebs*, who are responsible for preaching and teaching Islam, dispensing justice in minor matters, controlling political factions and reporting any extraordinary occurrences, such as the comings and goings of *don mihun*. And they are also responsible for managing the nearby uninhabited islands, unless of course these islands have been leased by the government (all land is State-owned) to some respected member of the community. When an island goes up for lease there is keen competition to acquire it, for there is a handsome profit to be made by sub-leasing the island or selling the produce, and paying as little as $30 per annum in rent.

For administrative purposes the islands are grouped into nineteen administrative atolls, with the capital island, Male, representing a separate twentieth division. These atolls are ruled by an *atolu verin* (atoll chief) and a number of *gazis*, who are responsible for the political, religious and economic welfare of the atoll.

Every day reports are sent via walkie-talkie from the island *kateeb* to the atoll office, and the *atolu verin* relays the relevant details via radiotelephone to head office in Male. Thus the national government, known colloquially as the "Male government", is always attuned to the day-to-day affairs throughout the archipelago.

At the apex of the political framework is the President, elected every five years by national referendum, after first being nominated by the *Citizens' Majlis*, or parliament, a body of fifty-four members comprised of two representatives from each atoll, eight from Male and eight Presidential nominees. Once nominated, the single candidate for President is invariably elected (via secret ballot) since the people vote simply yes or no. Also, because the constitution stipulates that the President shall have supreme authority to propagate the tenets of Islam throughout the Maldives and *sariatu*, or Islamic Law, is the only legal code, few people ever dare to vote "no".

Religious beliefs

For the past eight hundred years Islam has been the backbone of Maldivian society. And so strong and rigid is the belief in Islam that any non-Moslem is regarded as a "non-believer" and can never become a citizen or marry into the society.

At an early age, every child is taught the Arabic alphabet, and by the age of five or six, most children can quite easily chant verses from the Quran. Until their mid-teens they will attend the local *makthab*, where the *kateeb* gives lessons in Arabic intoning and Islamic history. An affluent few may attend the Atoll Community School or one of the English-medium schools in Male where Islam is studied in depth.

Despite this, however, the *Divehin* are moderate rather than fanatical Moslems, belonging to the largest Islamic sect, the Sunni sect, and practising the liberal Shafi'i rite. Here, unlike other Moslem communities, the women do not observe purdah and criminals are punished none too severely. Indeed nowadays the most brutal form of physical punishment is a light flogging with a *duraa*, a taut leather strap. But during Amin Didi's reign in the 1950s thieves did have their hands cut off. This, along with Didi's other fanatical measures, such as his ban on smoking and his instruction that the people eat leaves when rice and flour were scarce, soon brought the people to revolt. Didi was mobbed and stoned, and he died soon afterwards. Today the most common form of punishment is to be placed under house-arrest, either briefly or for a number of years, or to be banished to a faraway island, exiled from family and friends. But as many visitors have noted, crime in the Maldives is rare, for fear, suspicion and superstition pervade the entire archipelago. On the whole, the *Divehin* may be regarded as "good Moslems", as most of them adhere to the basic obligations of Islam, namely:

repeating the creed, La ilaha illa Allah, Muhammed rasul Allah — There is no God but Allah, Muhammed is the messenger of Allah.

praying five times a day

fasting for a month every year, during the daylight hours

giving a donation to the poor

making the pilgrimage to Mecca, at least once in their lifetime if they can afford it.

In every village there are at least two mosques, one for the men, the other for the women. Some are new, others centuries old. Some are made of coral, others of thatch. And all are meticulously cleaned and cared for by the local *mudeem* (muezzin), who summons the people to prayer at dawn, then again at midday, mid-afternoon, sunset and nightfall.

Attendances at the mosque are usually quite small, though most people often utter a short prayer or practise *namaad* at home or on board their *dorni* (fishing boat). And on Fridays almost every man and young boy will don his whitest *mundu* (sarong) and *gamis* (shirt) and head off to *Hukuru namaad* at the local mosque.

And beyond the typical *namaad* prayer, most families engage in a *salavat* or *maalud* on some special occasion. For example, when a child is born, a group of four or five men may be summoned to the house to recite some lengthy Moslem lore, and many families regularly employ someone well versed in the Islamic scriptures to chant a *salavat*, so that the home will supposedly remain free of evil spirits.

Many *Divehin* are convinced that evil spirits, or *jinnis*, inhabit the sea, the sky, the bushes and the tops of houses and trees. In nearly every house, every night, the doors and windows are locked and a small kerosene lamp, a *fulibati*, is left burning to keep out the demons. Young and Christopher once remarked that the people are "sunk in ignorance" and "the most absurd and superstitious fancies exert a powerful and pernicious influence".

Everyday beliefs and ideals are easily explained by the Islamic scriptures, but superstitions and extraordinary events are left to the local magician, the *fandita* man. For instance, when the fish don't bite, or the crops don't grow, or when someone is sick, many people will look to *fandita*, a sort of religious science. Nearly every village can boast of someone who is trained in the art of *fandita*, someone who is able to concoct potions, philosophy and personal interest to combat (or invoke) the ever-present *jinni*.

Islam

Islam is the youngest and one of the largest of the world's great religions, having over one-third of a billion adherents, called Moslems.

The basic belief of this religion is that there is only one God, called Allah, and his final and most complete revelation was given to the prophet Muhammed, who was born in Mecca about 570 AD.

During his formative years, Muhammed rode camels across the Middle East and spent much of his time in the mountains around Mecca, pondering the fate of his people. At the age of thirty he was overcome, while meditating, with an ecstatic seizure. He was convinced it was a revelation from Allah. A series of similar fits followed over the next few years, then Muhammed began preaching to the Meccans, telling them that Allah was the only God — and he was not to be worshipped with idols.

This, of course, provoked outrage. The aged and the rich made their livelihood from the idols and images that decorated the Kaaba, the huge wall that had been built to protect a sacred black stone, a stone which supposedly fell from heaven in the days of Adam and Eve. Nevertheless, Muhammed continued to spread the word, until he was forced to flee, in 622, to Medina.

Here, Muhammed continued his preaching and made frequent small raids on Meccan caravans. Slowly he enhanced his wealth and influence. Then, in 630, he led a force of 10,000 followers into Mecca, destroyed the idols and images in the Kaaba, and virtually became the sole leader of the Arabian people.

Following his death in 632, Muhammed's revelations became the scriptures of Islam, the Quran, and some of his notable "sayings" comprised the hadith.

But as Islam spread across several nations there developed variations in certain beliefs and practices. Broadly speaking, two sects evolved.

Eighty-five percent of all Moslems attempt to follow the path of their religion as laid down by the prophet and the first four successors, the "orthodox caliphs". These Moslems are known as traditionalists, or Sunnis. The large majority of the rest maintain that the real leaders of Islam are the twelve descendants of Ab, the prophet's son-in-law, the last of the "orthodox caliphs". The twelfth descendant disappeared in 878 and the "Partisans of Ali", the Shi'ites, believe that someday he will return to lead Islam into a golden age — hence the popularity of such people as Ayotollah Komeini!

Within each sect, also, there are further divisions. The Sunni sect, for example, embraces four schools of thought. The most conservative practitioners are called Hanabalites, and they are found all across Saudi Arabia. A little more tolerant in their practice of Islam are the Moslems in Upper Egypt and Syria, a "group" known popularly as the Malikites. Those in the Maldives, and in India, Indonesia, Lower Egypt and Syria, are called Shafi'ites and believe that some form of judicial speculation is a necessary and valid addition to the Quran and hadith in the application of *sariatu,* or Islamic law. The most "liberal" of all Moslems, however, are found in some parts of West Asia, India and Lower Egypt, and they are known widely as Hanifites.

Classes of society

In days gone by it was considered dishonourable to eat with a member of an inferior class, or to sit in the company of a superior other than on a low stool. The superior class were the *befalu*, the Sultan and his relatives, and they all bore titles like *Maniku* and *Didi*, and prohibited anyone without a permit to wear shoes, buy a flashlight, erect a fence around his house or even to study a foreign language.

Nowadays, however, things are a little different. "More civilised", Bell would say. *Maniku* and *Didi* are popular nicknames, *Kilegefanu* is the most coveted title, something like a knighthood, and is bestowed only on a handful of people, including the President. And *Kalegefanu* is bestowed on anyone, commoner or otherwise, who renders outstanding service to the community .

The most overt form of social distance today is found in the language, with different words and phrases adopted according to whom one speaks. To a fisherman, for example, one simply says *aharen* for "I", but to a government official one says *alugandu*, meaning "slave self".

Respect, today, is measured not only by one's political friends, but also by personal wealth and, to a lesser extent, education. Of course the capital houses the greatest number of influential people, but on the far-flung islands there are also many highly respected citizens whose status is measured according to the number of boats they own or the islands they lease.

The rest of the population is ranked, traditionally, according to the work they do.

Fishermen comprise the largest peer group, nearly fifty per cent of the total workforce. And within this group the *keolu*, or fishing crew captain, is the most highly-paid, earning about one-fifth of the day's catch, which, during a good fishing season, may be as many as a thousand fish. Not surprisingly, it is fish, be it tuna or skipjack, that accounts for nearly half the national revenue, as most of it is canned locally and sold to Japan, or cooked and dried, or salted, and sold to Sri Lanka, India and further afield.

It follows, of course, given that the lifeblood of the islands is fish, that the passport for survival for most people is a fishing boat, or *dorni*. Built from coconut wood and local hardwood, these *dornis* resemble sleek Arab-like dhows as they carve through the water with their lateen cloth sails. Those who build them, the *maavadi mihun*, are widely regarded as artists, despite their age-old techniques and tools.

A team of four or five carpenters can hand-carve, in just forty days, the standard family man's *dorni*, which is about ten metres long, built to last up to fifteen years — and costs only $US1000. Almost every family owns at least one small *dorni*, others may have several, plus a couple of longer boats — *mas dornis*, *batelis* and *vedis* — some twenty-five to thirty metres long, perhaps with an engine and usually with a thatch or wooden deckhouse for sheltering cargo during long-distance voyages.

And on the same social rung as the *maavadis* and *keolus* are the medicine men, the local *hakeems*. Throughout the archipelago there are some one hundred and seventy *hakeems*, held in high esteem by the village community. They use herbs and natural ointments and profess age-old family techniques coupled with a Unani philosophy of medicine. An assortment of leaves, nuts, sticks and seeds is ground to produce a prescribed *Divehi bes* (medicine). Basically the *hakeem's* philosophy suggests that good health is a product of the proper balance between the hot, cold and dry "humours" in the body, so *hiki mas*, or dry fish, is usually prescribed for flu and millet or betel leaf, or some such "cold food" is recommended to patients with a fever.

Of the part-time occupations, weaving coir and thatch are the most widespread. In every village, women and young girls can be found making rope and cadjan, to sell on the local market, or to repair their house or family boat. And down in the southern atolls, the women are renowned for their outstanding fine reed mats which are often used to decorate the local mosque or family furniture.

Elsewhere there are craftsmen who specialise in making gold and silver jewellery, or carving lacquered boxes.

On the bottom rung of the social scale are the *raaveri*, who earn their living by tending the coconut trees and tapping the sap.

And in a class all of their own are the *Giraavaru* people.

Festivals and holidays

Whilst most Asians celebrate auspicious occasions with frivolity and fanfare, the Maldivians celebrate theirs by feasting and fasting. Gastronomical feats accompany all the major religious festivals, while organised sports and speeches mark most historical anniversaries.

Rorda mas the fasting month, is by far the most outstanding national event. Everyone, except those too young or too sick (which includes pregnant and menstruating women), or those so daring as to cheat, abstains from all food, water, cigarettes and sex for an entire lunar month, the month of *Ramadan,* from sunup to sundown. The days are slow and the tempers short. Should someone even dare to smoke a much desired newspaper *bidi* someone else on that island would smell it, and the culprit would be banished. By sunset the women and young girls have prepared a wondrous spread and at the sound of the *sangu* (hornshell) the evenings become gay and gastronomical. Everyone dashes for a *kurumba* (drinking coconut) and follows up with *sā* (tea) and short-eats. Around 9 or 10pm it's mounds of rice and relays of curries, then sleep, only to be woken a few hours later to squeeze in one last meal before dawn.

And the days go on and on, until the end of *Ramadan*, when the new moon is sighted. Everyone then rejoices by sacrificing a chicken and wearing a new set of clothes. And the rich give a donation to the poor. It is **Kuda Id**.

Then, exactly two Moslem months and ten days later, anyone who is able and affluent joins the pilgrimage to Mecca, while others stay home to celebrate **Bodu Id** with another chicken dinner.

In terms of gastronomy, Prophet Muhammed's birthday is a highlight each year. In almost every village, for three days, families beckon each other, and you, at any time of the day or night to *ade kaan* — come and eat! No matter how poor the family, they offer an assortment of dishes with anything from *roshi* and *mas huni* to breadfruit and banana chips.

National Day is spectacular, and affords an opportunity to see the sights you will miss if you don't have time for a prolonged tour through the atolls. Men, women and children are presented in traditional costumes as they walk in a glittering parade through the main streets of Male, and in the National Stadium there are official speeches, military displays and a variety of traditional dances. And crowds of people line the fences and rooftops for a better view of the parade. This day, December 17, commemorates the overthrow of the Portuguese in 1578.

November 11 is the anniversary of the second **Republic** and June 26 is the anniversary of **full independence**, and both are celebrated by a modest fireworks display and government speeches. Other not-quite-so-renowned national anniversaries include **Huravee Day** commemorating the overthrow of the Malabaris in 1752, and **Martyr's Day**, honouring the death of Sultan Ali VI in 1558.

Closer to home, on the family level, there are a number of special occasions. When a child is seven days old, a name is designated, and close friends join the family for a *maalud* and meal. When the boys are six or seven years of age they are circumcised, and such an event demands plenty of food, festivity and loud music over several days. The tenets of Islam also require much attention to the death of a family member. For a week or more, special prayers will be said beside the graveside and at home, and on the fortieth day a memorial service, or *faatiha*, will be conducted over a lengthy *maalud* and sumptuous food. Families will have a *faatiha* on the same day every year, sometimes for several generations of the dead.

Marriage and divorce

Beside fishing, religion and gossip, marriage and divorce are the most popular pastimes. At one time, it was considered a mark of some pride and piety for a man to be married many times, and better still if he could afford four wives at once. Still today it is not uncommon to find people who have been married ten or twenty times — a distinguished citizen in Male has been married eighty-nine times! — sometimes to the same partner.

The male can be divorced simply by saying "I divorce you", then reporting the matter to the local *gazi*, and though the women are a little more restricted and can initiate divorce only on the grounds of cruelty, desertion or adultery, the Maldives can still lay claim to the highest divorce rate in the United Nations — eight out of ten people are divorced at least once. Therefore it is hardly surprising that the marriage ceremony is a rather simple affair. In fact the bride-to-be does not even attend her own ceremony, instead the groom and the father or uncle of the bride formalise the matter with the *gazi* and two witnesses at the local court house. On some occasions, young, newly-married couples may arrange a *kaveni sā*, a small reception with *sā* and short-eats and a few hours' dancing, not unlike a frivolous, carefree children's birthday party.

Music and dance

Given that children are brought up to regard conservatism, self-control and suppressing emotions as the accepted norm of society, it should not surprise that self-expression through music, or dancing and singing, is somewhat limited in style.

The traditional dance is little more than a swinging of arms and legs in gay abandon to the rhythmic beat of a *bodu beru* (drum). But when the beat nears its climax, some dancers fling themselves into a frenzy, some even go into a trance. The most outrageous dance is the *tara*, in fact so outrageous that the government has now banned the climactic scenario where the dancer jabs his head with an iron spike until blood flows. Nevertheless, it is said that some people in the northern atolls still practise the *tara* in its entirety — behind closed doors.

The most popular dance is the *bandia jehang*, performed by groups of young girls swinging their bodies as they tap a rhythm on metal water pots. Equally widespread is the *dandi jehang*, involving similar movements by groups of men tapping the rhythm out with tiny sticks.

The most popular form of song is the *raivaru*, a sort of poetic lament which may be sung in the company of a friend or lover, to the family at home or to the crew on a *dorni*. Quite often it is dedicated to love or happiness or loneliness, or simply a philosophy on life. It is a rare experience to lie back on the deck of a *dorni*, far out to sea, and listen to the old man at the helm sing a *raivaru*. "*Vadi a neti ge Kaashi-dhoooo . . .*" echoes from most *dornis* that cross the infamous Kaashidhoo *kandu*.

Island food

The *Divehi kotu* (island food) is not, by any stretch of the imagination, a banquet, but considering so few ingredients are available, the people can provide a tasty, interesting unique cuisine.

The staple diet is rice and *garudia* (fish broth), and though it may appear bland and boring to the newcomer, the taste is immediately enhanced by a dash of *rihaakuru,* a thick, salty fish paste, or an *assara,* a small spicy side-dish of onion and lime, or pickled papaya.

Another popular dish is *roshi* (unleavened bread) and *mas huni*, a salad mixture of grated coconut, dry fish, lime and spices, which is eaten as a snack or a meal. There is also a wide range of mild, creamy curries made from home-ground curry pastes, fish and locally grown vegetables, such as breadfruit, pumpkin, sweet potato and eggplant.

But for most visitors the highlight of the local cuisine is the short-eats — small sweets and savouries with names like *gula, keemia, kavaabu, borkibaa* and *foni foli* —best eaten with the national beverage, *sā.*

A few easy recipes to prepare for yourself are:

Mas huni

  1 onion
  1 fresh chilli
  1 lime
  pinch of salt
  250g freshly grated coconut
  250g fish (flaked dry fish, tinned tuna, cooked fish — cold)
  Optional: finely chopped herbs (fresh parsley or coriander)

Mix finely diced onion and chilli with lime juice, then grind in the remaining ingredients with your hand. Serve with roshi.

Roshi

  500g flour
  200g freshly grated coconut
  pinch of salt
  water

Mix ingredients, make a well in the middle and slowly knead in the water until the dough is firm and doesn't stick. Divide into four balls and roll out into large, fairly thick circles. Cook each side on a hot metal surface (no oil). Serve while hot, one per person, with a bowl of mas huni.

Barabor riha

  500g pumpkin, cubed
  1 onion, chopped
  4 cloves of garlic, sliced
  1 tablespoon fresh coriander, chopped
  2 fresh chillis, mild
  2 teaspoons cinnamon
  1 pinch fresh ginger
  ½ lime
  2 tablespoons oil
  salt to taste
  250g fish (flaked dry fish, fresh tuna, tinned tuna)
  2 tablespoons curry powder, or mix your own: 3 teaspoons cummin, 2 teaspoons fennel, 1 teaspoon ground coriander, ½ teaspoon tumeric and a good dash of black pepper.

1 whole coconut, grated: Just cover the coconut scrapings with water and squeeze with your hand into a milk. Drain off the milk and keep to the side. Repeat the process twice more, mixing the second and third milk together and keeping the first and thickest milk separate.

Heat your saucepan and fry a small part of the onion and garlic in the oil, until soft. Using a wooden spoon, fold in the pumpkin, along with the ginger and half the leftover onion and garlic. Cover the pan, lower the heat and cook until the pumpkin is a little soft, stirring occasionally. Pour in the thin coconut milk and add remaining onion, chillis, curry powder, fish, and salt to taste. Simmer slowly until pumpkin and fish are cooked, adding water if necessary. Fold in remaining garlic, fresh coriander, cinnamon and lime juice. Simmer a further 3 minutes, with the lid on. Remove from heat and fold in the thick coconut milk (coconut cream can be used instead). Serve lukewarm, with boiled rice or roshi, so that it can be eaten with the hand.

Sä-eche

There are some real treats in the Maldives and among the best is the array of savoury and sweet short-eats that decorate the tea-shop tables. The *kuli eche,* or savouries, are usually based on a mixture of dried smoked tuna fish, grated coconut, lime juice, onion and chilli. And the *foni eche,* or sweets, are simple concoctions of flour, sugar and eggs, and sometimes a few generous slurps of coconut honey.

First, a selection of *kuli eche* to whet the appetite:

fihunu mas fish brushed with curry paste and cooked slowly over hot coals.

gula fish mixture wrapped in a pastry ball and deep fried

kavaabu deep fried fish rissole

keemia deep fried fish roll, the local answer to the Aussie sausage roll

kuli bis fish mixture wrapped in oval-shaped pastry, steamed, turned in a thick, creamy curry paste and eaten with a spoon

kuli borkibaa mildly spiced fish cake

samosa fish mixture wrapped in triangular shaped pastry, deep fried, and with a slightly sweet after-taste

telali bambukeo breadfruit chips

telali kavaabu fish rissole wrapped in yellow batter and deep fried

telali mas chunks of fish brushed with a chilli-onion-garlic paste and fried.

And next, to complete the gastronomy, a choice of *foni eche:*

banas   small bread rolls (there are various bakeries spread around Male), usually served with jam

bondi   white, finger-long coconut stick. Other varieties, wrapped in leaves, can be found in the market stalls

bondi-bai   rice custard

foni borkibaa   gelatin-like cake

foni foli   thick pikelets

keku   fluffy, plain cake

kastaad   custard, served on a saucer. Very sweet

rorst paan   slices of bread dipped in egg and sugar, and fried

suji   cereal drink, made with semolina and coconut milk, a few sultanas and *kanamadu* nuts, sugar and a dash of cinnamon and cardamon

telali bambukeo   strips of breadfruit, deep fried until golden brown on the outside and mushy in the middle. Naturally sweet.

Island language

The language spoken almost uniformly through the Maldives is called *Divehi*. It is closely related to Elu, an ancient form of Sinhala, and contains a smattering of Arabic, Hindu and English words.

Given the wide geographical dispersion of the islands it is not surprising that some vocabulary and pronunciation may vary from island to island, indeed it varies significantly as one moves to the south, towards the equator. Here, there are three distinct dialects of *Divehi*, each similar in stress and intonation but having quite different words and phrases. In the north, for example, rice is *bai* but in the south it is *bate* or *ba*.

And, as mentioned, there are different words and phrases within the various classes of society. In fact there are three "levels" of *Divehi*, with the highest, the *reeti bas* or nice language, being used in the company of the upper echelon and also on national radio and television, and the lowest being used by the masses.

Along the well-worn tourist tracks and deep down in the south, around Gan, where the British once lived, you can get by quite easily using English, but in the far-flung villages you should be armed with at least a few *Divehi* phrases. For a useful guide, refer to the chapter on "The Maldivian language".

And if you're keen you may care to learn *Taana*, the local script. Like *Divehi* it's not difficult to learn, in fact eight out of ten locals can read and write, which is hardly surprising given that there are only twenty-four letters in the alphabet and nine of them are Arabic numerals. And vowels are represented simply by a dash above or below the letter.

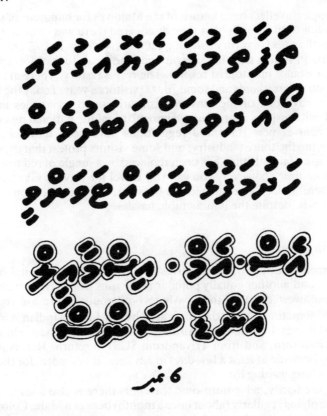

Taana was invented during the sixteenth century, soon after the overthrow of the Portuguese, when the locals were determined to revive their faith in Islam. Unlike the earlier scripts it was written from right to left to accommodate Arabic phrases, now commonplace in the island language.

Facts for the visitor

Although travellers have known of the Maldives for hundreds of years it was not until recently that they discovered there was more to these islands than *hiki mas* (dry fish) and temporary wives. In 1972, George Corbin, an Italian traveller, encouraged the locals to transform some of their islands into tourist resorts. The rest is history. There are now fifty-odd resort islands and some 70,000 visitors a year. Today the Maldivians have one of the most tourism-orientated economies in the world, with visitors contributing almost 20% of the national revenue.

Of course, new rules and regulations have been introduced to streamline the tourist industry, and some visitors protest that the original laissez-faire attitude has been replaced by a jungle of red tape. At the same time, however, you can still travel for travel's sake and go anywhere, indeed you can become Moslem, marry and live on one of the islands, despite the innumerable hassles.

Getting there

The main gateway to the Maldives is at Colombo, the capital of Sri Lanka, and another equally popular route runs from Trivandrum, on the southwest coast of India. Along both routes there are regular flights, sometimes every day, operated by Air Lanka, Indian Airlines and Maldives International Airline. From Colombo the flight costs $US146 return, and from Trivandrum $US116 return. Reservations should be made at least a few days in advance, if not more, for there is often a long waiting list.

For the hardy, adventuresome travellers there is also a sea-freight service plying regularly (about once a month) between Male, Colombo and Tuticorin (southeast of Trivandrum) and the sixty-hour voyage costs only $US35 one way, meals included. It is by no means comfortable, nor very convenient, but it is an experience long remembered. In short, you rough it!

Information regarding arrivals, departures and passage formalities can be obtained from Pioneer Shipping Agencies, 676 Galle Road,

Colombo 3 (tel: 87746). In Tuticorin, along South Raja Street, there are a number of contacts: V.V. Danushkodi Nadar & Sons (tel: 20038), S. Albert & Co. (tel: 21276) and Kumanar & Co. (tel: 21926). And if you care to make the return voyage, look for the owners/agents around the market streets in Male — Enif Ocean Services, Marine Export Co., Huvadu Shipping, Matrana Enterprises and DIK are worthwhile contacts.

It is also quite easy to hitch a ride as a working crew-member on one of the dozens of yachts that sail around Southeast Asia, across to Sri Lanka and on to the Maldives. The typical route is Bali-Singapore-Pangkor-Penang-Langkawi-Phuket-Sri Lanka-Maldives, and then most head on to the Red Sea or down to South Africa.

From Southeast Asia, however, the quickest route is a four-hour direct flight from Singapore with Singapore Airlines, costing about $S1250 return — if you book a month in advance and stay a minimum of five days or a maximum of 30 days. Or if you prefer an enroute stopover in Sri Lanka, a number of airlines, notably Air Lanka and UTA, make regular flights to Colombo for about $S850 one way.

From Australia there are two flights a week, operated by Singapore Airlines, leaving all the major cities, stopping off in Singapore then flying on to the Maldives. A number of travel agents offer package deals on these flights for around $A1000 — return air fare plus 8 days on a resort — but the only fault with these packages is that you arrive at night and hence miss out on the awe-inspiring aerial view of the islands. For around $A800 the best alternative is to fly British Airways to Singapore, or KLM, once-a-week, from Sydney or Melbourne direct to Colombo. Then Air Lanka for the rest of the journey.

From Europe there are various alternatives. Between November and April there are chartered flights from Frankfurt, Paris and Rome to the Maldives, and there are regular scheduled flights with Singapore Airlines from all the major cities — about DM2500 one-way from Frankfurt. And Aeroflot have a scheduled service planned, from Copenhagen via Moscow direct to the Maldives. Or alternatively there are many regular services operating direct to Colombo.

From the United Kingdom the most popular route is a flight from London to Colombo, stopover for a few days, then fly on to the Maldives. British Airways, UTA and Air Lanka each provide regular services, and by checking-out the travel ads in the weekly *TNT International* publication, return London-Colombo Apex fares can be found for around £500.

From America there are no direct flights to the Maldives, so shop around for an air-ticket to London or Singapore for about $US1000 return, then continue on from there.

Travel agents who are reputed to offer popular tours to the Maldives include:

Sri Lanka

Aitken Spence	— *Sir Baron Jayatilaka Mawatha, Colombo 1. tel: 27861*
Gateway Holidays	— *148 Galle Road, Dehiwela. tel: 712183*
Gemini Tours	— *40 Wijerama Mawatha, Colombo 7. tel: 98446*
Hemtours	— *30/2 Bristol Street, Colombo 1. tel: 28796*
Mackinnons Travel	— *York Street, Colombo 1. tel: 29881*
Uniresort & Travel	— *77 Dharmapala Mawatha, Colombo 3. tel: 25032*
Walkers Tours	— *130 Glennie Street, Colombo 2. tel: 21101*

India

Taj Mahal Hotel	— *Apollo Bunder, Bombay. tel: 24 3366*

Australia

Australian Himalayan Expeditions	— *159 Cathedral Street, Woolloomooloo, Sydney. tel: 357 3555*

CBR Tours	— *123 Clarence Street,* *Sydney. tel: 290 3499*
Ceylon Tours	— *249 Pitt Street,* *Sydney. tel: 264 5895*
Club Mediterranee	— *388 George Street,* *Sydney. tel: 231 1811*
India-Ceylon Travel Service	— *104 Bathurst Street,* *Sydney. tel: 264 8700*
New Horizons	— *95 St. George's Terrace,* *Perth. tel: 321 7823*
Penthouse Tours	— *109 Pitt Street,* *Sydney. tel: 231 1455*
Peregrine Expeditions	— *343 Little Collins Street,* *Melbourne. tel: 60 1121*
Travel Action	— *83 Albert Street,* *Brisbane. tel: 229 7205*

Europe

Adventure Nel Mondo	— *via Cino da Pistoia,* *Rome.*
Daro Voyages	— *22 Rue Royale,* *Paris.*
Indiamex — Department Tourisme	— *7 Place Vendôme,* *Paris. tel: 296 1682*
Intur	— *via Bligmy 5,* *Torino. tel: 53 0863*
Manta Reisen	— *Meinrad Lienert-Strasse 5,* *Zurich. tel: 461 5577*
Voiles Voyages	— *8 Rue Domât,* *Paris.*

United Kingdom

| Interlink Holidays | — *18 Hanover Street,*
London. tel: 628 9581 |
| Penthouse Travel | — *35 Manchester Street,*
London. |

73°

Haa Alifu

Dhidhoo

Nolivaramfaru

Haa Dhaalu

Farukolufunadhoo

Shaviyani

Noonu

Manadhoo

Raa

Ugoofaru

Baa

Eydhafushi

Laviyani

Nailaru

Kaashidhoo

Channel

Kaashidhoo

Kaafu

Hulhule
MALE

Alifu

Mahibadhoo

Vaavu

Felidhoo

N
W E
S

0   40   80 km

Maldive archipelago

Equator 0°

Muli

Dhaalu

Kudahuvadhoo

Thaa

Veymandhoo

Laamu

Hithadhoo

One and Half Degree Channel

Viligili

Gaafu Alifu

Thinadhoo

Gaafu Dhaalu

Equatorial Channel

Fuamulak

Gnyaviyani

Hithadhoo

Seenu

73°

0°

On arrival flight passengers disembark on an island called Hulhule, or, more proudly, Male International Airport. It lies about 4kms, or ten minutes' boatride, northeast of the capital, and in close proximity to most of the resorts. Not long ago Hulhule was reserved for the Sultan and his friends, but today it is reserved for incoming and outgoing flight passengers, and those who hold a permit. So if you wish to visit the island or meet a passenger, a permit should be obtained from the Airport Authority in Male for Rf5. Outgoing passengers should note that a tax of Rf45 is to be paid on departure.

Hulhule, though not quite as lavish as other international airports, has all the necessary facilities, including a snack bar, a couple of boutiques, a bank and an information centre. And there is a regular ferry service to the capital for Rf5 and to the nearby resorts for $US5 upward, depending on the distance.

Exchanging formalities

Visas

Everyone — except Israeli citizens — is given a 30-day visa on arrival, and Indians and Bangladeshis are given 90 days, provided one holds a valid passport. And anyone arriving from a country known to be plagued with yellow fever or cholera is required to be properly vaccinated.

For extended visits, application should be made to the Department of Immigration and Emigration in Male, and on completing the necessary forms and presenting a passport photo along with your passport, a one, two or three month "tourist visa " may be granted the following day — at a cost of Rf300. However, like other Asian nations, the Maldives is somewhat cautious in granting these extensions, so a neat appearance and a patient, pleasant manner along with a reasonable reason as to why you want to extend your visit, will all prove worthwhile.

Permits

Anyone who intends visiting any village beyond Male must obtain a travel permit — available on request for Rf5 — from the Tourist Information counter at the airport or from the Ministry of Atolls Administration in Male. Such permits are issued, however, only to visitors who travel on an organised tour, as arranged by one of the resorts or registered travel agents, but you'd be well advised to list a number of alternative destinations, in case your travel plans are subsequently changed (due to weather for example), because upon arrival in any of the villages the island *kateeb* will usually scrutinise your permit, and demand that you leave if his island or atoll is not listed in your itinerary!

Customs

Time magazine once published an article suggesting that the Maldives was a "land of leisurely customs as unchanging as the sea". Be that as it may, travellers should be wary if they are tempted to arrive with a gram or two of grass concealed in their luggage. Gone are the days when you are greeted with a handshake and not bothered about passports. Today, local customs officers are by no means aloof, but they are well-trained and they hold a well-framed image of a so-called "hippie". A Maldivian once told me "a hippie is someone who wears long hair and carries a cloth bag". Many visitors have found themselves frisked, fined around $US1500, jailed if they can't pay, and deported.

Others should note that firearms, dogs and pornographic pictures are forbidden, and the Maldivians have strict ideas as to what they consider pornographic — *Playboy* is pornographic! Remember, too, that alcohol cannot be imported without an official licence, a licence granted only to the tourist hotels, resort islands and a few expatriates.

Modesty, too, demands serious consideration. Boobs and bottoms may be bared on the resorts, but around the villages and in Male certain standards are enforced. Women are asked to refrain from revealing more than they cover, hence a light, conservative summer outfit is considered appropriate. The "see-through" look is not appreciated, particularly in Male, and it invariably encourages embarrassing reactions, resulting in the *sifāng* (police) asking you to cover-up — or leave the island! Men, on the other hand, are requested to wear no more (nor less) than shorts and shirt, or the traditional sarong and shirt when visiting a village.

Another custom which often causes embarrassing looks relates to eating. If you choose to eat as the locals do — with your hands — remember never to handle food with your left hand. It's not a matter of simple manners here, but inviolable hygiene custom! And once the meal has begun don't handle the cutlery or crockery with your right hand — use your left. If it all sounds a little confusing then eat as the *befalu* do — with a *samsaa* (spoon).

MALDIVE ISLANDS

Even the Sharks are Friendly

Time, May 18, 1981

Tropical paradises are rarely heavenly, but the Maldive Islands come close. The 1,200 coral islands — "give or take a few", say locals — of the former British protectorate are often no bigger than a New York City block and usually an escapist's dream. Including the capital, Male, only about 200 are inhabited. The rest are pristine Edens of coconut palms and white sand surrounded by breathtaking underwater scenery. It is a nation of leisurely customs as unchanging as the sea. By a tradition at least 500 years old, even criminals are treated gently. The standard "punishment" is banishment to an outlying atoll. Yet for reasons bemused city dwellers may initially find hard to fathom, the sun-drenched vest-pocket republic is trying to pull itself into the 20th century.

The Maldive Islands, the peaks of a submerged mountain chain, form a 512-mile archipelago that stretches north-south across the Equator, some 300 miles southwest of India. It is one of the poorest countries in the world; the per capita income of its 146,000 citizens is no more than $160 a year. Fishing, primarily by the old hook-and-line method, accounts for three-quarters of the Maldives' $26.7 million G.N.P. Practically everything — including the main staple, rice — has to be imported at great cost. There are almost no natural resources of any consequence, including arable land. Fresh water is scarce. Thanks to cholera and infant dysentery, life expectancy is a mere 46.5 years. Still, the government of President Maumoon Abdul Gayoom, 43, has pieced together an ambitious development program touching everything from education to health care. His main weapons: a booming tourism industry and an active search for foreign aid.

Gayoom does have a magnet of sorts in his quest for international attention. Gan, the southernmost island in the Maldives, lies just 450 miles north of another, better-known Indian Ocean island: Diego Garcia. Moreover, Gan has an old military base, abandoned by the British in 1976, that contains an 8,700ft runway capable of handling just about any nation's military jets. In addition, it has hangars, permanent barracks, fuel storage tanks, a pier and such amenities as an 18-hole golf course and tennis courts, all in fairly good condition. Though it is of little use to the republic, Gan is a prime attraction for the superpowers jockeying for Indian Ocean influence. Their interest has not been reciprocated; an offer from the Soviets to lease the island for a reputed $1 million a year in 1976 was firmly rebuffed. "Our foreign policy is based on the principles of non-alignment and neutrality", the President explains. "We firmly support all efforts to make the Indian Ocean a zone of peace, free from big-power rivalries".

In an effort to head off a strategic tug of war over Gan, the Maldivians have tried a number of schemes to put the base to peaceful uses. One was to convert it to a tourist centre, but that was no good because the island, astonishingly, has no beaches. The current favourite is a plan to import 200 sewing and knitting machines from Hong Kong so that 500 Maldivians can turn out garments for export.

But, for the Maldives as a whole, the future bonanza seems to lie with tourism not commerce. Some 42,000 foreigners visited the Maldives last year — compared with 919 in 1972 — and the government expects an annual influx of 100,000 by 1985. Most of the visitors come from West Germany, Italy and France to stay at one of the 34 resorts, each occupying its own island. Though air fares from Europe are high, tourists are attracted by the reasonable rates of up to $100 a night with meals for two. And, of course, there are the beaches, the wind surfing, the water ski-ing, the sunbathing, the swimming and the other delicious pleasures of *dolce far niente*. Diving in the crystaline waters seems to be the favourite pastime, attracting cognoscenti from around the world. Spearfishing is forbidden, but that is only fair in a place where, as one islander puts it, "even the sharks are friendly".

With the stake from tourist income, Gayoom has assiduously cultivated international aid organisations like the World Bank and the United Nations and sought closer ties with fellow Muslims in oil-rich countries like Saudi Arabia and Kuwait. All told, the annual harvest of foreign aid amounts to about 10% of G.N.P. And the President has attracted a floodlet of advance men from international banks like Chase Manhattan and Citicorp. Ostensibly, the bankers go to study the islands' potential as an offshore tax refuge. But they always show up between November and February, when the climate is at its most gorgeous. Whatever their professional opinions, they doubtless agree with a West German tourist, who was sentenced to life banishment on an uninhabited island after murdering his girlfriend. He refused every attempt by his consul to bring him home to a West German jail.

—By Jay D. Palmer. Reported by Marcia Gauger/Male.

Currency

Foreign currency can be exchanged for local currency — *rufiya* and *laari* — only through authorised moneychangers, such as banks, resorts and some private shops. A black market does not exist.

The *rufiya* is the paper currency and appears in denominations of 1, 2, 5, 10, 50 and 100, while the *laari* is the coinage with denominations of 1, 2, 5, 10, 25 and 50. One *rufiya* is equivalent to 100 *laari*, and rates of exchange are linked closely to the American dollar, the most widely accepted foreign currency. Therefore prices quoted in this book, unless otherwise specified, are $US. Some popular rates, effective early 1985, include:

$US	Rf7.00	£E	Rf11.34
$A	5.40	frS	3.05
$C	4.79	DM	2.63
$S	2.97	Yen	0.02

There are no regulations regarding the import or export of foreign or local currency, and "plastic money" is accepted on most of the resorts. But be wary of the quality of local notes, as they are sometimes tattered, torn, and worthless. Exchange the worthless notes at one of the banks or at the Maldive Monetary Authority next to the Post Office in Male. And if you're bound for the villages be sure to stock-up on Rf1 and Rf2 notes, because often it is difficult to find change of a Rf10 note.

Places to stay

The government requests that every visitor stay at a registered resort, tourist hotel, vessel or guesthouse, where facilities are periodically checked to ensure they meet certain government-approved standards. And where a daily "tourism tax" of Rf22.50 is levied on every guest.

Most of these places are a matter of minutes or perhaps a few hours from the airport and, unless otherwise stated, the room rates quoted in the following pages include the so-called "$3 tax".

Resort islands
Most visitors spend their time on one of the fifty-odd resorts which are scattered around Kaafu atoll and the neighbouring atolls, where room rates for singles/doubles vary from $30/40 upwards, meals included.

The facilities are basically the same on every resort, though standards and ambience are somewhat varied. The catch-cry is "peace and tranquility", and the setting is thatch-roof coral cabanas around the fringe of the island, a restaurant, bar and boutique centrally located, and a diving school providing facilities for various types of watersport — diving, snorkelling, windsurfing . . .

The rooms are fan-cooled with bathroom attached, and some may have a refrigerator and air-conditioning. The restaurants offer pre-arranged western or local-style meals, snacks on order, and the bar stocks a variety of imported beers, whiskies and wines. And the boutiques sell local souvenirs, imported Asian handicrafts and clothes, Kodak and Agfa film at good prices, cosmetics, posters and postcards.

During the sunny, dry northeast monsoon, from November till April, the resorts are bursting with tourists escaping the European winter, so reservations need to be made well in advance. Due to the excess of guests, however, most resorts are confronted with a perennial problem — a shortage of "fresh" running water. The underground fresh-water reservoir becomes depleted and brackish, so rainwater is precious and usually preserved for cooking and drinking. For many visitors it's no big deal — the salty shower is all part of the Robinson Crusoe atmosphere, but for others it's a hassle, particularly when the water supply is pungent. Some may therefore care to note that the Universal and Taj resorts, and the Nika Hotel are renowned for their desalinised water.

During the southwest monsoon, from May till October, when the skies may pour sunshine, showers or squalls, the tourists are few and far between, the fresh-water wells fill up, some resorts close down and others slash their rates (up to 25% off) to attract the trickle of visitors.

Tourist Hotels

Tourist hotels are found only in Male — two are foreign-owned and two are "government guesthouses". They are the capital's answer to star-class comfort, though on an international scale they would each rate, if any, one-star.

The rooms are fan-cooled — with air-conditioning if you want it for $15 a day extra — and have bathrooms attached. And there's a licensed restaurant serving a la carte meals. Rates for singles/doubles vary from $30/40 upward.

Vessels

A wide range of sea-faring craft, including imported schooners, ketches and cabin cruisers and locally-built *yacht-dornis*, are available for hire and approved by the government to be suitable for accommodating tourists. Most of them provide either cabins or bunks for groups of eight to ten passengers — or even more at a squeeze — with cooking and toilet facilities and a crew of two or three local sailors. The usual charge, including meals, varies upwards from $30 a day per person, with an additional charge levied for the hire of scuba-diving equipment. The resorts and the travel agents in Male can arrange a short or long-distance island-hopping tour on a registered vessel.

Guesthouses

Anyone planning to visit the Maldives on a shoestring budget should perhaps think twice. Visitors are now prohibited from visiting any of the villages beyond Male, the capital, unless they want to pay tourist prices and join an organised tour on a registered vessel, or unless a *rajje miha* (island person) is willing to testify that you are a *rātehi* (friend), or preferably a *rahumatehi* (a very close friend). You may find a sponsor among the former guesthouse proprietors who nowadays depend on fishing or selling souvenirs. But, frankly speaking, your chances are slim.

So be warned: If you're on a light travel budget you will inevitably spend most of your time in Male, where a sparsely furnished fan-cooled room, or at least a camp bed and communal *gifili* will cost around Rf40 a day.

Island pastimes

Given that it usually takes less than half an hour to explore the length and breadth of most islands, one is tempted to ask "What is there to do in the Maldives?". Invariably the answer is: not much! In fact, it is the very art of doing "not much", except basking in the crystal clear lagoons, that attracts thousands of visitors to these islands every year.

However, there is a simple calendar of amusements offered by all the resorts to satisfy those who are quickly frustrated by the "peace and tranquility". Volleyball and badminton are popular pastimes, tennis courts are available on some resorts, and after dark most resorts have a disco or *bandia jehang*, or a lobster barbecue on the beach. Night fishing, too, is a great way to while away the hours and trolling a line over the deck of a *dorni* on the nearby reef generally guarantees a few metre-long surgeons and groupers, to be enjoyed later on as a midnight snack. Such fishing trips usually cost about $7 per person.

And a half-day excursion to Male from any of the resorts can easily be made for around $8, or for a similar price you can sail across to visit one of the nearby fishing villages where you can get some idea of the local lifestyle and bargain for local handicrafts.

But, of course, it's the water sports that capture most visitors. Windsurfers are available on all the resorts for about $7 an hour, and some resorts also offer hobie-cats, paragliders and water skis for about $10 an hour. Snorkelling equipment can be hired for around $3 a day and scuba gear is available to anyone who cares to explore the deep-sea caves, caverns and shipwrecks, or watch the resident diving instructor hand-feed the sharks and moray eels.

You could travel almost anywhere in the Maldives and be enraptured by the underwater scenery, but of course the better-known destinations are found around Kaafu atoll, a $6 boatride from most of the resorts. From September till April visibility in these waters is between 40 and 60 metres, and from May till August it is reduced to around 20 metres due to the plankton bloom.

Sweetlip, surgeons, grouper, Queen triggers, rainbow runners and a variety of parrot fish are common sights around the fringing reefs of most islands, a short paddle from the shore, and Jackfish turrum, mackerel and reef sharks are often seen during deep-sea dives. And during the plankton bloom whalesharks and manta rays can always be found.

The following list of diving spots will give some idea of what one can expect to find around most coral reefs.

Banana Split a 20 metre high, cone-shaped reef peaking 3 metres below the surface. It is close to Furana and a popular spot with novice divers.

Kandu Giri the outer reef near Kadu Oiy Giri, the chicken farm, is enmeshed in soft corals, houses shoals of sweetlip, red bass, coral trout and grouper, and is a popular rendezvous with professional underwater photographers.

Maagiri situated a few minutes' boatride northwest of Furana is a series of caves renowned for their profusion of gorgonia, magnificent fan-shaped corals.

Maldivian Victory named after the government's cargo ship which sank off Hulhule in February, 1981 — on Friday 13th to be exact! Still today the seabed is littered with umbrellas and cassettes from Singapore. With care, the diver can quite easily explore the cabin areas and the holds. The ship lies in about 40 metres of water and is buoyed for easy access.

Manta Point the outer reef wall beyond Lankanfinolhu is known for its manta rays, some of them 3 metres wide.

Shallow Point near Baros, is a reef with an ever-present school of barracuda.

The Entrance situated between Furana and Farukolufushi is an undulating terrain with several gullies and gradual drop-offs, a profusion of clownfish amidst superb yellow and pink sea anemones and burrow upon burrow of garden eels.

The Opera House only a few minutes' boatride from Bandos is an amphitheatre of overhangs and shallow caves protecting thousands of colourful reef fish and the ever-present shark and turtle.

Veligadu an uninhabited island near Kuramathi in Alifu atoll, is an arena for hammerhead sharks.

Veteran diving enthusiasts can hire equipment for about $170 a week and novice divers can enrol in a basic scuba diving course for about $115 a week, or have a single test dive accompanied by a professional instructor for $20.

In order to learn to dive, you need only be capable of performing the following water skills without swimming aids. These skills are the minimum prerequisites and, usually, you will be required to demonstrate them at the first session.

— Swim 200 metres non-stop using two or more types of stroke. Form and comfort are more important than speed.
— Swim at least 12 metres underwater on a single breath of air.
— Dive to a depth of 3 metres, recover a 2 kilo object, and swim the object to the surface.
— Tread water for at least five minutes.
— Float, drownproof, or bob with a minimum amount of movement for at least five minutes.

Getting around

Five hundred years ago, according to Joao de Barros, "you could hop from island to island by swinging from the branches of trees". Today you can island-hop by chartering a plane or planning an organised tour or, perhaps best of all, by hitching a ride on any one of the thousands of *dorni* that are forever criss-crossing the archipelago.

By flying

You can charter a three-seater Cherokee or a five-seater Cessna from the Airport Authority in Male, but it's not cheap — around $160 (Cherokee) and $320 (Cessna) an hour. A cheaper alternative is the two-hour flight from Hulhule to Gan, in the southern atoll, on a 17-seater Skyvan. It is operated twice a week by Air Maldives, the domestic airline, for a return fare of Rf900 (Rf750 for locals). Reservations should be made well in advance.

Also in the offing, perhaps operative before the end of 1986, are scheduled flights from Hulhule to Laamu, Noonu and Haa Alifu atolls.

By an organised tour

From every resort you can island-hop on half-day excursions to the neighbouring villages, and some resorts have their own speed-boats and launches which are available for hire.

MTCC, the Maldive Trading and Contracting Company, a government-owned organisation, and **Ocean Sport**, a Swedish company, are both well-known for their fleets of speed-boats, varying in cost from $8 an hour to $300 a day, not including petrol. They're handy contacts for those in a hurry, or anyone requiring a boat on-the-spot for a private tour.

Voyages Maldives is by far the most highly reputed travel agency in Male. It offers popular budget tours and cultural expeditions, provides access to a wide range of *yacht-dornis*, schooners and ketches, and arranges air-tickets and resort accommodation. Among their outstanding offerings are the *Baraabaru,* a magnificent 17-metre *yacht-dorni,* the brain-child of its French owner/captain who has spent many years in the far-flung islands, and the *Hagern,* an imported, old-time 24-metre schooner. Both offer comfortable cabins and facilities, are best suited to groups of ten or less, and charter for around $50 per person per day, meals included. Similarly priced, though a little smaller is the *Jacoba Catharina,* one of a half-dozen 13-metre sloops available through Voyages. Then there is a selection of smaller *yacht-dornis,* each providing reasonable comfort for any type of tour.

Universal Enterprises owns the *Thakandhoo,* another old-time schooner that has been refurbished to provide comfort for tour groups, and it too is a great way to travel if you can afford about $50 a day, per person.

Safari Tours provides tours on board the *Safari Queen,* the former

Sultan's launch. Costs are around $33 a day per person, with meals included. And for diving enthusiasts scuba tanks are available for an extra charge.

Laaba Travels also have a speed launch, the *Lady Marina,* which is adequate for groups of six or seven and priced at $60 a day per person, with meals and all the necessary diving equipment included.

Cyprea Limited is a worthwhile contact if you're looking for a big, reasonably priced *yacht-dorni.* The *Anbaara* is 16-metres long, has 14 bunks, the usual small kitchen and toilet, and rents for around $300 a day, food and diving equipment included.

And cheaper still are the 12 to 14-metre *Akiri* boats, available through **Akiri**, on Marine Drive in Male. They are best suited to groups of four, have been known to squeeze in seven, and can be yours for less than $100 a day, if you provide your own food.

Similarly priced *yacht-dornis* and a couple of cabin-cruisers can be found at **Quest Enterprises**, operators of one of the most popular resorts, Ihuru.

There's virtually no end to the list of possibilities. Name it, and most times it's either available or can be arranged. A worthwhile exercise is to contact each of the travel agents in Male and have them provide a description of what they offer. Many of the popular tours and boats are solidly booked-out well before the start of the high season (November till April), so make enquiries well in advance. A list of agents and their addresses can be found in the "Male" chapter.

By hitching

If you're bound for one of the resort islands and prefer to experience an adventure not to be found on the resorts' ferry service, you might be tempted to travel on one of the *dornis* which are anchored in the local Male harbour, just around from the Post Office. There are hundreds of them preparing to set sail for the nearby and far-flung islands. And if their route takes them via the resort of your choice you could probably hitch a ride for a small negotiable fee. In the old days, when one could go wherever one wanted to (whether on a registered tourist vessel, or not), hitching by dorni was not so unusual. Of course there's no form of timetable as everything depends very much on the wind and current, so it may take a few hours or even several days to get where you're going, but you can be sure that the experience will be long remembered — even if you pay twice the local fare (around Rf30

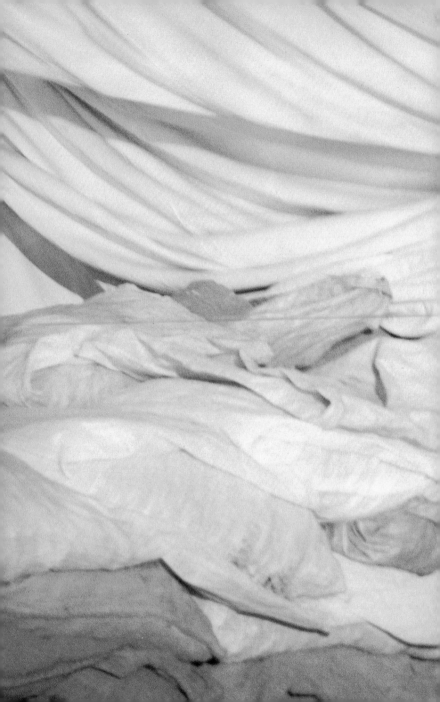

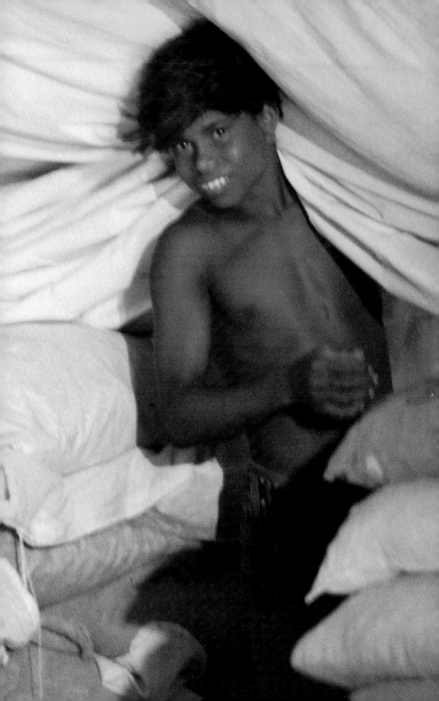

should get you to any of the resorts in Alifu, for example). But be prepared, there can be hassles.

As mentioned before in this book, many *rajje mihun* look upon *don mihun* with fear and suspicion, so the crew on these *dornis* might simply stare and refuse to speak to you, or perhaps totally ignore you. Or indeed, they might even make a few empty promises. For instance, having been promised a lift it would not be unusual to arrive at the wharf with your luggage, and find the *dorni* already gone, or with no intention of leaving until *maadama* (tomorrow). Hitching a ride involves patience and a great deal of perseverance. A few words of *Divehi* will never go astray (nor will a packet of cigarettes handed around to all on board), because Maldivians immediately warm to anyone who shows an interest in their language and customs.

The comforts, of course, are minimal. You simply huddle between the bags of rice or balance on the thatch-roof deckhouse, and sometimes you'll get wet, cold and frustrated, other times you'll be forced to squat at the stern, precariously balanced over the edge to perform your natural duties. These voyages are only for hardy, adventuresome travellers and not for those who are easily aggravated by discomfort.

And remember to stock up on a few short-eats and sundries if you're bound for a far-flung resort, which might take over a day to reach, as rice and boiled fish can become monotonous.

If you're determined, you will invariably succeed in getting a lift. All you need say is *kong rajje ti dani?* (which island are you going to?) and, if it's close to your destination, reply *gengos denang ta?* (will you take me?). The problem, obviously, lies in understanding the response, so an interpreter is a wise idea. And you can easily confirm where a *dorni* is bound simply by checking the number on the bow. Each *dorni* has a number like 4077-7E, and the letter indicates the atoll to which it belongs. From north to south through the archipelago the *dornis* will be labelled as follows:

A Haa Alifu	F Baa	K Meemu	P Gaafu Alifu
B Haa Dhaalu	G Laviyani	L Faafu	Q Gaafu Dhaalu
C Shaviyani	H Kaafu	M Dhaalu	R Gnyaviyani
D Noonu	I Alifu	N Thaa	S Seenu
E Raa	J Vaavu	O Laamu	T Male

If hitching a ride on the local *dornis* is too much to handle, try getting to and from the resorts via the so-called "supply *dornis*". Every resort has one, and it makes daily return trips to Male to fetch fruits, fish and vegetables at the market — and you can arrange a lift simply by chatting-up the crew. Then after a swim and lunch you can hitch back to Male the same day — or stay overnight.

General information

Consulates, embassies and information offices

Countries which have diplomatic relations with the Maldives usually operate their consular offices from Colombo in Sri Lanka, though some also have offices in Male. See the "Male" chapter for addresses.

The Maldives, in turn, has a consular office, or at least a consultant, in Sri Lanka, Germany and the United Kingdom, and from each some scant tourist propaganda may be available. The addresses are as follows:

Sri Lanka	High Commission,
	25 Melbourne Avenue,
	Colombo 4,
	Sri Lanka. tel: 86762
Germany	Consul,
	Immanuel-Kant-Strasse 16,
	D-6380 Bad Homburg v.d.H.,
	West Germany.
United Kingdom	Consultant,
	Glebe House, Welder's Lane
	Chalfont St. Peter,
	Buckinghamshire,
	United Kingdom.

The Maldives Department of Tourism provides an information counter at the airport and an office in Male, where a list of resorts and guesthouses and perhaps a few maps can be obtained. And there is some quite good literature available at the Department of Information and Broadcasting, and a selection of historical works at the libraries in Male.

Health

In the past, a great many travellers have succumbed to the infamous "Maldive fever", and though it's not widespread today many visitors recommend a weekly malaria tablet. Others suggest you carry a reliable mosquito repellant, such as citronella oil or *madiri dundandis* (mosquito coils). A vaccination for yellow fever and cholera is required if you're arriving from any country plagued by such a disease, and some people will tell you that a vaccine against typhus and tetanus is wise when travelling anywhere in Asia.

Bear in mind that the average life-span in the Maldives is only 50.5 years, due largely to intestinal diseases and a very poor diet — those on the poverty line often exist on rice and sugar, and few people ever eat vegetables — so really any number of vaccines is unlikely to prevent some small stomach complaint. Be wary. Avoid drinking water from the island wells — rely on boiled water or rainwater, or better still ask for a *kurumba* or some deliciously sweet *raa* (toddy). There are Atoll Health Centres in every atoll and if you feel like flushing your system try *anti-paa,* a sweet peppermint syrup available from most island stores — or try chewing very slowly on a papaya leaf — it seems to cure most stomach upsets.

An equally common problem for visitors is sunburn. Some form of protection is essential, even for the bronzed skin sun-worshippers — don't underestimate the rays, particularly when you are travelling by *dorni* when you can so easily be fooled by the sun and the soft sea breezes. And sunglasses, too, are a must for protection against the blinding glare that bounces off the white sand and white-washed coral buildings.

Time and business hours
The Maldives is five hours ahead of Greenwich Mean Time, so when it is 12 noon locally it is 12.30pm in India and Sri Lanka, and 5pm in Sydney. It is 2am in New York and 7am in London, and in San Francisco it is 11pm the previous day.

As with all Islamic nations, every Friday is a holiday, and though shops and restaurants close only for noon prayers (from 11am till 2pm), government offices are closed for the entire day, opening every other day from 8am to 1.30pm. The Post Office is open every day, except Friday, from 7.30am to 1.30pm and 3 to 5pm. Banks however, operate only from Sunday to Thursday from 9am to 1pm. And most retail shops, other than those in the main bazaar that close at 6pm, continue working all day, every day, closing at 10pm.

During the month of fasting, *Ramadan,* working hours are staggered or shortened, or in some places non-existent.

Post and telecommunications

Mail to and from anywhere in the world takes up to 10 days, but parcels sent surface-mail take 6 months or more. In fact, sending parcels of gifts or souvenirs out of the Maldives is a somewhat laborious affair, since a customs officer is obliged to check the goods and invariably he is confronted by a sea of eager Indian businessmen all pleading for attention. Allow, therefore, at least half a day in the post office if you are sending parcels overseas, and if what you are sending just happens to be some sort of local handicraft, or is made of gold, silver or brass, then it must be cleared at the Customs Office, around the block from the Post Office. Here you must complete some forms and, if any of the goods exceed Rf20 in value, pay a tax — receipts are not necessary. For lacquered boxes, or any wooden products, the tax is 15%, and for jewellery made of black coral or turtle shell it's 20%.

And remember that any incoming mail sent to Poste Restante, Male, will be held for two months only.

Philatelists will love the colour and variety of Maldivian stamps and, if you're truly interested, a fine old collection can be viewed in Male at Raiyvilaage, 10 Fareedhee Magu, near Novelty Bookshop.

Phone calls and telex messages can easily be sent to any part of the world, from Cable and Wireless in Male or from any of the resorts. But from the villages one can contact only neighbouring islands via walkie-talkie, or distant islands by radio-telephone.

Electricity

Those travelling to the fishing villages and far-flung islands should not rely on electrical appliances — kerosene is the main source of current. However, on the resorts and in Male, plug fittings of the round-pin British type are available and power is 240 volts, alternating current and five cycles. But the small power plant that provides current to Male's population is more often than not stretched to its limits, so it's not unusual for the island to have frequent blackouts and for air-conditioners to be out-of-order during the midday heatwaves.

Photography

The professionals will tell you one thing about the tropics: beware of the heat. It soon ruins your film, so always keep it in a clean, cool place, and remember that the best photos are taken before 10am and after 3pm and usually with a polarising filter.

Most locals are only too eager to be photographed (they'd love you to send them a copy) and in fact it doesn't take a group of ten or more kids more than a few seconds to gather before your lens. There are, however, two places which demand respect from photographers — taking close-ups of people at prayer in a mosque, particularly in Male, is frowned upon and it's forbidden to take close-ups of Muleeaage, the President's official residence.

Film processing in Male is offered by Cento Foto on Majeedi Magu and Fototeknik on Ameer Ahmed Magu, and films for prints and slides are available at a number of stores in Male and on the resorts, at reasonable prices.

Tipping

The official policy regarding tipping for services is advertised on a billboard at the airport: Tipping is prohibited. But the unofficial policy is, of course, whatever you decide. You are rarely asked for a tip, but there is one resort, which suggests — in a list of "do's and don'ts" — that "tipping is your generosity". In the tourist resorts and hotels a service charge rarely applies, so most guests automatically make a small donation to their room-boy or waiter. But in the local tea shops and guesthouses, *sukuria*, or thank you, is more than enough — in fact it is very rarely heard.

Investments

Since the birth of the tourist industry in the Maldives, many foreign investors have shown a keen interest in leasing an island, constructing a resort and reaping the benefits of tax-free profits and duty-free imports. Of course there are certain guidelines to adhere to, and there are as many failures as there are success stories. Information can be sought from the Ministry of Shipping and Foreign Investment, in Male.

Media

There is only one local newspaper, the eight-page, stencilled *Aa Fathis*, which contains a few paragraphs of English news. However, the Department of Information often publishes a bulletin in English, covering the outstanding local occurrences. The international magazines, *Time* and *Newsweek*, are available every week at a few shops in Male and on some of the resorts.

The prime media outlets are radio and television, one of each and both are government-controlled. The Voice of Maldives broadcasts from 5.30am to 10.30pm every day, and though the bulk of the programmes are in the *Divehi* language with Hindi love-songs, there is the occasional English pop record and a news bulletin in English at 6pm every day.

TV Maldives operates from 7pm to 8.30pm every day, except Friday when it operates from 6pm to 9pm. The programmes are a mixture of Quranic recitals, local plays, Hindi movies and the occasional *Sesame Street* or *Charlie's Angels*.

There are also a number of privately-owned cinemas in Male, but the usual fare is some sticky-sweet, action-packed, Hindi musical. If you've never seen one, here's your chance.

Shopping
A wide selection of domestic handiwork can be found around the islands, and from November 11 to 18 each year, in Male, there's an exhibition of the best local work, all available for sale at quite reasonable prices — although most quality products are reserved for the government ministers and various *befalu*.

Of course it's always best and cheapest if you buy from the source, though you may also manage a quite good deal by shopping-around the tourist shops in Male and the nearby villages. The prices are always negotiable, except at the exhibition where price tags are applied.

Some of the souvenirs you are likely to come across might include:

Jewellery Brittle branches of black coral are plucked from the deep by island divers. You can't export black coral in its natural state but the veinous branches are cut and polished then set into rings, earings, pendants, bangles and jewellery boxes.

In the central atolls there are a few jewellers who specialise in gold and silver, but none of it seems quite as beautiful as the jewellery made by their ancestors, which is still readily available today — intricately carved heavy silver bracelets and armlets, long thin silver-mesh belts that wrap several times around your waist, silver charm boxes, gold chains and necklaces.

Turtle shell Turtle's shells are made into all sorts of decorative items, but there is nothing more delightful than seeing this beautiful shell float past you underwater, on the back of that busy little bald-headed creature. And there is nothing so soul-destroying as seeing these magnificent, unassuming animals die a slow and sordid death on their way to the market-place. Any temptation to purchase turtle-shell wares would be dampened once you experience first-hand the process involved in obtaining the shell.

The government now prohibits the capture of smaller-sized turtles, and though there are stuffed adult turtles, shell and all, on sale in Male, they cannot be taken out of the country.

Sea shells There are thousands of shells along the island shores. Cowries and nautilus shells are abundant. Conch, pearl and trident shells are rare. All can be bought in the tourist shops, either in their raw state, or beautifully polished.

Wooden boxes Among the most popular purchases are the hand-carved lacquered boxes which are made in Baa atoll. They come in various sizes from a pill-box to boxes used for carrying a family feast to the mosque, and all are lacquered in strands of red, black and yellow and finely etched with an abstract design.

Mats Women from villages in the northern and southern atolls weave fine reed mats, the most outstanding being the *tandu kunaa*, either two-metres long or place-mat size. They are woven on a hand-loom using a locally-grown reed which is dried and naturally dyed various shades of cream, caramel, brown and black, and, depending on the intricacy of the Islamic design, they will sell for around Rf60 at the source, or up to $60 from shops and touts in Male.

Musical instruments The *bodu beru* is made from a hollowed piece of coconut wood with the hide of a sting-ray enclosing each end. They are available from a few of the tourist shops, and in any village one could offer ten or fifteen dollars and be sure to find a good quality drum.

Materials The Maldivians have their own fashions: the *mundu* and *gamis* for men, the *Divehi hedung, libaas* and *kandiki* for women (see "Glossary"). And for some unknown reason these island people, living so close to the equator, choose to make their clothes out of brightly coloured print-polyesters — though some of the older generation still prefer the brown and cream locally-woven *feyli* cloth, made in Baa atoll.

The *mundu* is worn and sold everywhere, but the *Divehi hedung* and *libaas* are custom made by the island tailors. In Male there are tailors along virtually every *magu* (street), some of them dabbling in safari suits and *fatalungs* (trousers), others in cheap cotton travel gear. And around the bazaar you may find a newly-made or old cotton *libaas* with intricate gold or silver embroidery, and everywhere there are bolts of imported cottons and synthetics, all very cheap.

And for $2 you can have a T-shirt emblazoned with your personal motif — a *dorni*, a sunset or an underwater scene.

Hiki mas The rock-hard fish, known popularly as *hiki mas* or "Maldive fish", is made by boiling and smoking fillets of tuna, then drying them under the sun for several days. Locally they are regarded as a source of nourishment and in neighbouring countries they are considered something of a delicacy. In Sri Lanka the merchants around the Colombo markets are known to pay up to four times the cost price for a kilo of "Maldive fish" and tourists are permitted to export up to four kilos when they leave the islands. You can find it in bulk in most of the villages, either from the local store or someone's kitchen, and it usually sells for around Rf10 a kilo.

Ambergris For hundreds of years the Maldives has been famous for its ambergris — from the gut of the sperm whale. It is an important ingredient in the manufacture of expensive cosmetics and perfumes, so finding a glob of this white, grey or black plasticine-like substance on the island-shore — often during the *hulungu* monsoon — is rather like winning the lottery. One kilo fetches around $1000 on the local market, and ten times that overseas. If you find some and care to export it, there's a 50% customs tax.

Local oddities If you're a collector of knick-knacks, scout around the back streets of the Male markets, and look for the "junk shops". There are only a couple, small and unassuming, but inside you'll discover a conglomeration of local inventions. And each one has a stamp of usefulness, be it for a sojourn in the outer atolls or a decoration for your mantelpiece. *Aibatis, fulibatis, taakias, hika fās, . . .*

Imported wares Around the Male bazaar you'll find an assortment of imported cosmetics, cassettes, calculators and watches, all at near duty-free prices (about 35% mark-up).

Male

Male — pronounced mar-leh — is the capital island, the business and political centre of the Maldives. Since the days when Koimala Kalo first settled on the island nearly 2000 years ago, until the Sultanate was finally abolished in 1968, Male was affectionately known as the "Isle of Sultans". It was the home of the elite *befalu* and the intellectual.

According to the most notable academic on Maldivian history, H.C.P. Bell, "Male, with its own quaint self-centred ways, is in certain respects an Oriental Utopia" but it is also an "architectural eyesore . . . a hideous medley of smugness and utilitarianism" and it is "teeming with a population of 5,200".

One wonders what Bell would think of Male today, just sixty years after his *Report on a Visit to Male.* On arrival one no longer gets the impression, as Bell did, of a "typical Asian village disclosing a long line of thatched dwellings and tropical vegetation", but instead, following Amin Didi's headlong program to modernise the island in the 1950s, one sees a maze of unpaved coral *magus, golhis* and *higuns,* and a profusion of white-washed coral houses, shops, offices and mosques adorned with rusting, hot, corrugated iron roofing. The village atmosphere does still exist in the outskirts, where the *Giraavaru* and poor people live — women still collect water at a communal well and gossip with their neighbours over the palm-latticed fence, and as the men bring home a fish from the bazaar everyone along the street calls out to find out how much he paid — but in the more sophisticated sections, the people are fanatical about privacy so they build their houses behind high coral walls. Indeed there are some beautiful old rambling houses with cool dark gardens found in many parts of the island, but in his enthusiasm to build wonderfully wide *magus* Didi thought nothing of destroying Male's trees. One could easily get sunstroke and eyesore exploring the island.

And one can only imagine Bell spinning like a top in his grave if he knew that Male now housed a permanent population of around 30,000 people, not to mention the 10,000 or so casual visitors who arrive from the nearby and far-flung villages, to trade at the only produce market in the country, and live for a few days on the deck of their *dorni* in the local harbour. Keeping pace with this ever-mounting population has required years of dredging, draining and filling-in the lagoon, until Male is now, in fact, two islands — known originally as Athamana Hura and Kuda Male — measuring nearly two square kilometres.

But surprisingly the visitor never sees Male as grossly over-populated — as one so readily sees Colombo or Madras — because the locals here are an excessively clean and tidy people. Not a speck of rubbish is found along any street, as it is all used for reclamation work in the southwest corner of the island or, unfortunately, ends up floating out to sea. And the majority of women are usually housebound, some visiting the bazaar at night perhaps once or twice a year, others claiming never to have seen the other end of the island.

For many *don mihun,* particularly those who are bound for the outlying villages, Male is the crossroad. And for others who prefer to patronise the resorts, Male is at least worth a visit, if only for an hour or two.

For ease of orientating oneself to the island, and traditionally for administrative purposes, Male is best viewed in terms of *avarus,* or suburbs. Henveiru is most noted for its two-storey government offices along the Marine Drive waterfront, some beautiful old *befalu* homes with overgrown gardens along Ameer Ahmed Magu, a host of guest-houses and close proximity to the best swimming spot on the island — if you don't mind side-stepping the broken glass and general refuse. Here, close to the Voice of Maldives, many locals enjoy a midday swim before *Hukuru namaad* but *don mihun* should carefully note that unless you enjoy a rowdy crowd of goggling onlookers it's best to swim as the locals do — fully-clothed.

Galolhu embraces a small, overly-compact residential pocket near the southeast corner of the island, and exploring this *avaru* is not unlike wandering through a mirror-mazed rabbit warren.

Maafannu extends from the bazaar and market across almost the entire western end of the island, embracing Theemuge, the President's private residence, several embassies and most of Male's poorer inhabitants.

And the fourth and final *avaru* is Machingolhi renowned for its concentration of tea shops festooned along Majeedi magu, the largest and widest street on the island, passing from east to west straight through the centre.

Places of interest

For most visitors, Male's most outstanding attraction is the hustle and bustle around the bazaar and market streets, and down along the local harbour. All day, every day — except during *Hukuru namaad* — tonnes of local produce, particularly *rornu* (rope), *fang* (cadjan) and *mas* (fish) and imported provisions such as rice, flour and sugar, are loaded and unloaded from *dorni* to dock, amidst clamorous bickering and bargaining.

And close by, around and along Chandani Magu, is the so-called **"Singapore bazaar"** where a score or more of *vihafari verin*, or businessmen, with names like DIK, SEK, and MAD, trade imported synthetics, cosmetics, cigarettes and electrical wares, and a half-dozen reputable travel agents offer programmed tours and accommodation on nearby resorts.

But for an historical appreciation of the island, stroll along Meduziyaarai Magu, beyond and behind the "Singapore bazaar". Here you will find the remains of the former Sultan's Palace — nowadays called **Sultan Park** — and near the small garden of trees and flowers is the **National Museum**, housing a scant but interesting collection of artifacts and archaeological finds. Admission to the park is free and it's open every day from 8am till 6pm, and on Fridays, when hundreds of locals congregate there to pose for the family album, it's open from 4pm till 6pm. Admission to the museum is Rf5.

Beside the park is the Earth Station and beyond that lies the **Hukuru Miski**, the most outstanding mosque in the country, adorned, sadly, with a brand-new corrugated iron roof. It was build in 1656 and inside are some ancient intricate engravings — but before entering, non-Moslems should seek permission from the Ministry of Religious Affairs. In 1667, a huge cylindrical tower, or *munnaru*, was built close by and until recently the island *mudeem* would scurry to the top and summon the people to pray. Of course nowadays he uses a loudspeaker, as do the other *mudeems* who cry out, simultaneously, from each of the thirty-odd mosques that are scattered across Male. The sound is not, unfortunately, even remotely similar to the spiritual, heart-wrenching wail that is heard in other Moslem communities in, say, Turkey and Pakistan. It is more like a piercing scream!

Around the most venerated mosques are meticulously preserved graveyards with the ancient tombstones of local heroes. Around the Hukuru Miski there are a number of gold-plated tombstones belong-

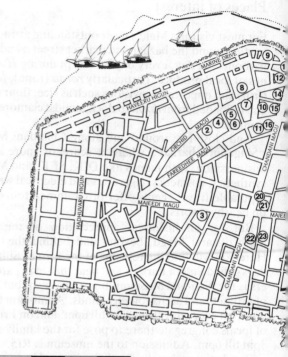

LEGEND

```
0        200        400 m
```

Airlines

Air Lanka	⑩
Air Maldives	㉗
Indian Airlines	㊲

Banks

Bank of Ceylon	⑫
Bank of Maldives	㊱
Habib Bank	⑭
State Bank of India	㊵

Consulates and embassies

American Consulate	㊼
Indian Embassy	⑦
Sri Lankan Embassy	④

Emergency services

Central Hospital	㊻
Police	㉙

Government offices

Airport Authority	㉖
Atolls Administration	㉔
Customs Office	㉕
Foreign Affairs	㊳
Ghaazee Building	㉘
Immigration & Emigration	㊺
Office of the President	㉟
Post Office	⑬

Libraries and bookshop

Asrafee Bookshop	②
MID Library	㊴
National Library	㉜
Novelty Bookshop	⑥

Places of interest

Fish market	⑨
Hukuru Miski	㉞
Muleeaage	㉛
National Stadium	㊶
Singapore bazaar	⑱
Sultan Park	㉚
Theemuge	⑧

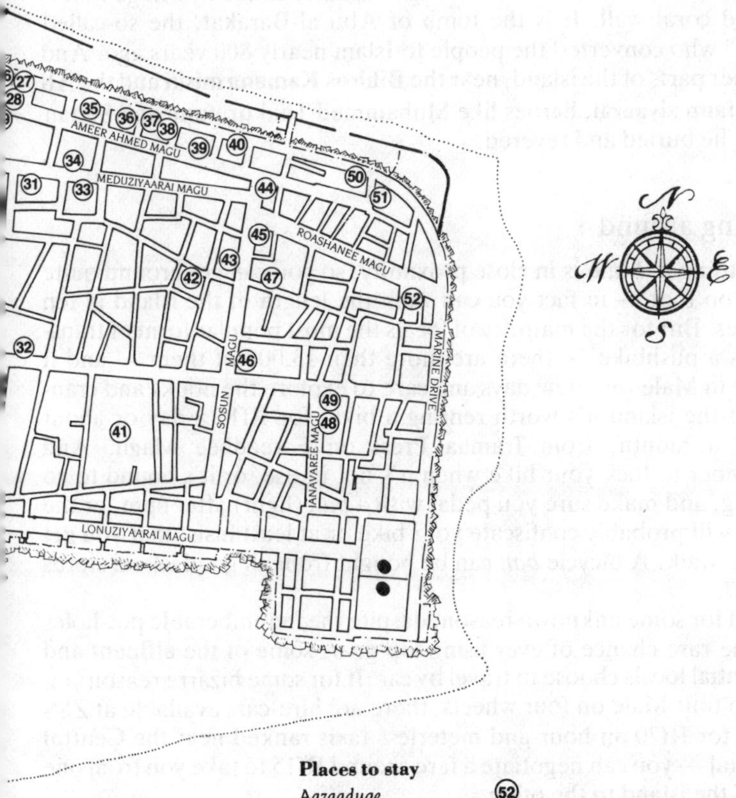

AMEER AHMED MAGU
MEDUZIYAARAI MAGU
ROASHANEE MAGU
MARINE DRIVE
SOSUN MAGU
JANAVAREE MAGU
LONUZIYAARAI MAGU
27 28 31 32 33 34 35 36 37 38 39 40 41 42 43 44 45 46 47 48 49 50 51 52
N E S W

Places to eat

Evening Glory 49
Gabbiano Gelato Italiano 16
Ice Ge 5
Majeedi Ufaa 21
Night Star 3

Places to stay

Aazaaduge 52
Blue Haven 44
Haji-Edhuruge 42
Hotel Alia 1
Mazaage 23
Nasandhura Palace Hotel 50
Nivico 22
Sakeena Manzil 31
Sony 48
Sosun ge 43

Telecommunication

Cable & Wireless 19

Travel agents

Imad's Agency 20
Quest Enterprises 51
Safari Tours 15
Universal Enterprises 17
Voyages Maldives 11

Antenna ●

Male

ing to former Sultans and members of the *befalu*, but the most outstanding tombstone is the **Meduziyaarai**, opposite the *munnaru*, festooned with medieval-like white flags and surrounded by a huge whitewashed coral wall. It is the tomb of Abu al-Barakat, the so-called "saint" who converted the people to Islam nearly 800 years ago. And on other parts of the island, near the **Bihiros Kamana miski** and the **Ali Raskefanu ziyaarai**, heroes like Muhammed Thakurufanu and Sultan Ali VI lie buried and revered.

Getting around

Everything in Male is in close proximity, so you can get around quite easily on foot — in fact you can walk the length of the island in ten minutes. But for the majority of locals the most popular form of transport is a pushbike — there are more than 13,000 of them — and if you're in Male for a few days and care to explore the nooks and crannies of the island it's worth renting a bike, for Rf15 a day or about Rf100 a month, from Iramaa Press on Fareedhee Magu. And remember to lock your bike when it's not in use, or it's bound to go missing, and make sure you pedal with a *bati* (light) after 6pm, or the *sifāng* will probably confiscate your bike or at least insist that you get off and walk. A bicycle *bati* can be bought from all good island stores for Rf7.

And for some unknown reason, despite the innumberable pot-holes and the rare chance of ever using top-gear, some of the affluent and influential locals choose to travel by car. If for some bizarre reason you care to tour Male on four wheels, there are hire-cars available at ZSS Tours for Rf70 an hour and meterless taxis ranked near the Central Hospital — you can negotiate a fare around Rf15 to take you from one end of the island to the other.

Places to stay

Visitors coming from the airport are met in Male by a rank of *aigaadias* (pushcarts) and any one of the "pushers" will willingly direct you to a nearby hotel or guesthouse, and transport your luggage for a negotiable fee — begin bargaining around Rf10. Or better still ring-up a few places from one of the nearby shops or public phone-booths, to ensure there are vacancies and suitable rates, before you go tramping off on a goose-chase for spare rooms. However, finding somewhere to stay is really no problem, because Male offers a wide range of guesthouses and a handful of tourist hotels and they're all quite clean, cheap and comfortable.

The **Alia Hotel** (tel: 3445) on Haveeru Higun, at the western-end of the island, is known amongst local expatriates as "The Pub". It's a popular meeting place, offering a cool palm-covered open-air bar where you'll often meet interesting people. And there's an air-conditioned restaurant serving a la carte meals and the occasional cheap buffet lunch, but the service is usually sleepy. The hotel has 17 rooms with singles/doubles costing around $32/42, and from here you can organise accommodation on a nearby resort or hire a speedboat or cabin cruiser for the day.

The **Nasandhura Palace Hotel** (tel: 3380) on Marine Drive, at the eastern end of the island, is a large white building — not unlike the hospital — with cold, clinical decor and a small stuffy bar. The restaurant, however, offers a good range of western meals and the service is quick and quite professional, and some of the 28 rooms have a harbour view with singles/doubles around $35/45. Here, accommodation on nearby resorts can easily be arranged.

The two government guesthouses are along Sosun Magu, close to the Central Hospital, and both offer a homely atmosphere which appeals to many visiting diplomats and VIPs. **Blue Haven** (tel: 2572), a large airy house, has four spacious rooms all with fan, fridge and bathtub, and singles/doubles around $38/51. **Sosun ge** (tel: 3025), is more austere and more expensive, with ten rooms and a palm-covered verandah, and singles/doubles around $46/74.

For the cost-conscious, the choice of accommodation is wider, with fifty-odd privately-owned registered guesthouses scattered across the island and priced to suit varying demands.

Among the most popular, for any type of budget, is **Aazaaduge** (tel: 2095) at 4 Roashanee Magu in Henveiru, close to the waterfront and the Nasandhura Palace Hotel. A small single room with communal bathroom costs around Rf40 a day and a larger double with attached bathroom costs only Rf50. The owner, Kuda Thuthu, is renowned for his helpful, reliable advice and trustworthy service.

Should it be full, and often it is, there are equally good rooms close by, at **Reedhoo Kokaage** (tel: 2505), at 5 Fiyaatoshi Golhi, with bed and breakfast for singles/doubles costing between Rf42/84 and Rf70/112, depending on the season. If it's too expensive (and for what you get, it is!), the owners, ZSS Tours, can direct you to cheaper-style accommodation. Or try Malam International (tel: 3389), a popular contact amongst travellers looking for cheap accommodation.

Some popular cheapies, particularly with the Indian clientele who demand very little in the way of comfort and convenience:

Sakeena Manzil (tel: 3281) on Meduziyaarai Magu, is a charming two-storey house close to the bazaar, adjacent to the Earth Station. Amidst a loud, jolly atmosphere, a dormitory bed and three meals a day costs Rf52 per person.

Saeeda Manzil (tel:2743) on the same *magu* as "sister Sakeena" has several small rooms with basic facilities and a boisterous atmosphere.

Nayaa Bahaaru (tel: 2866) at 15 Violet Fehi Magu in Henveiru, opposite the American Consular Agency, has five small dark rooms with communal facilites, and costs around Rf40 per person.

Haji-Edhuruge (tel: 3351) on Hithifiniva Magu in Henveiru, close to the Iraqi Ambassador's residence, is one of the largest guesthouses in Male, having eight spacious fan-cooled rooms, attached or communal bathrooms and a reputation for great Indian food. Room rates vary upward from Rf42 per person.

Glory Aage (tel: 3067) on Faamudheyri Magu, behind the "Singapore bazaar", has three small rooms, communal bathroom and costs around Rf40 per person.

Ocean Reed (tel: 3711) on Fareedhee Magu, opposite Voyages Maldives travel agency, has dormitory beds for Rf35 a day.

Boaniyoa on Hadhuvaru Higun, near the Id Miski, a well-known landmark in Male, has a large dormitory room with four beds and a self-service kitchen. Rates are around Rf32 per person.

Fehi Vidhuvaruge on Funa Golhi, opposite the Reno Cinema, has a few claustrophobic rooms, a communal *gifili* and hours of bellowing Hindi music for Rf30 per person.

Mazaage on Nikagas Magu, a short walk from some outstanding tea shops, has several good rooms with rates around Rf42 per person.

There are also a number of up-market guesthouses, all over-priced but worth remembering if you're only in Male overnight.

Sony (tel: 3249) on Janavaree Magu in Henveiru, near the popular Evening Glory restaurant, has four rooms above a grocery shop with prices for singles/doubles varying from Rf56/98 to Rf72/126, depending on the whim of the shopkeeper. It's quite popular with travellers — and you can order room service if you wish.

Nivico (tel: 2972) on Chandani Magu has seven rooms, also above a grocery shop, and lies close to a host of popular eating places. Rates vary upward from Rf43 per person.

Ranmahi (tel: 3362) on Lonuziyaarai Magu in Gololhu has four small clean rooms with singles/doubles costing Rf110/225, including meals. One of the attractions here is the owner's promise to give guests a complimentary tour of Kadu Oiy Giri, a nearby uninhabited island used to raise poultry.

Mermaid Inn (tel: 3329) on Marine Drive, near the Alia Hotel and overlooking the local harbour, is a two-storey house with ten rooms, attached bathrooms and a small unlicensed restaurant. Singles/doubles cost Rf140/210.

Places to eat

Along almost every *magu, golhi* and *higun* you're bound to find a tea shop close by, and while most offer *sā* and a variety of short-eats, others provide rice, *roshi* and curries at various times of the day. The tourist hotels provide cosmopolitan cuisine.

However, Majeedi Magu houses some of the most popular places to eat. In Henveiru, the **Evening Glory** is famous for its *gulas, kavaabus* and *borkibaas,* and opposite is **The Crest**, noted for its fried fish and chilli-hot vegetable curries. But still more popular, particularly with *don mihun,* is the **Majeedi Ufaa**, close to the major Chandani-Majeedi Magu junction, where a variety of short-eats and mild vegetable curries are available almost any time of the day. And beyond the junction, down towards Maafunu, is the **Night Star**, an Indian restaurant which specialises in paratha, dahl and chicken curry.

In any and all of these places a few *rufiya* at most is enough to bloat-up on short-eats and *kalu* (black) *sā* and a dollar or two usually ensures a small feast of rice, curry and a few side dishes. And despite the fumes from the kitchen, the heat and the noise, it's quite easy to be enthralled by the action in one of these tea shops. As soon as you enter the table is strewn with an assortment of short-eats, *kalu* and *kiru* (milk) *sā* is always on tap and the atmosphere is a constant buzz of conversation and music. But don't be surprised at the reaction when you sit down, particularly if you're a woman, for the locals will often shuffle to another table rather than sit with a *don miha*. Then, no sooner have you finished your *sā* than the waiter begins clearing the dishes, counting what's left of the short-eats and charging twenty-five or fifty *laari* for each *sā-etche* consumed.

Along Chandani Magu also there are a couple of outstanding eating places. **Semi's Cinema** offers fan-cooled "VIP rooms" for those who care to pay a service charge for their *sā* and short-eats, and **Food City** provides an a la carte menu, attractive decor and exorbitant prices. Still more outstanding, and more expensive, is **Gabbiano Gelato Italiano**, near Voyages Maldives, where gelati, sandwiches and spaghetti are served in a thatch-covered garden. It's well worth a visit.

For anything cool and cheap, such as canned drinks, iced coffee and sundaes, most travellers head for **Ice Ge**, an air-conditioned restaurant near the Indian Embassy on Orchid Magu, or down to the waterfront, to the **Cool Spot**, near the Bank of Maldives.

The night-life

The hedonists looking for the pleasures of Bangkok and Manila will be none too impressed with the night life in Male. It is distinctly sleepy. Apart from the experience of a Hindi movie showing at one of the half-dozen cinemas or whiling away the hours over a gelato or *gula,* the most popular after-dark pastime is *hama hingani* — just ambling and browsing along the main *magus*. Or once in a while there may be a live disco at Ice Ge or Food City, or at one of the tourist hotels.

Some useful addresses

Airlines

Air Lanka,
Faamudheyri Magu. tel: 3479

British Airways,
Voyages Maldives,
2 Fareedhee Magu. tel: 2019

Balair,
Imad's Agency,
39/2 Chandani Magu. tel: 3441

Condor,
Universal Enterprises Ltd.,
15 Chandani Magu. tel: 3510

Indian Airlines,
Sifaa,
Marine Drive,
Henveiru. tel: 3004

Maldives International Airline,
Sifaa,
Marine Drive,
Henveiru. tel: 3003

KLM Royal Dutch Airlines,
Speed Travels,
1/1 Fareedhee Magu. tel: 3069

Singapore Airlines,
Sisal Corner,
3/5 Faamudheyri Magu.

LTU,
Maalethila,
Henveiru. tel: 3202

Banks

Bank of Ceylon,
Orchid Magu. tel: 3045

Habib Bank,
Chandani Magu. tel: 2052

Bank of Maldives,
Marine Drive. tel: 3095

State Bank of India,
Marine Drive. tel: 3054

Consulates and embassies

American Consulate,
Mandhuedhuruge,
Violet Fehi Magu,
Henveiru. tel: 2581

Pakistani Embassy,
Moonimaage,
Lilly Magu,
Galohu. tel: 3005

French Consulate,
S.E.K. No. 1,
Chandani Magu. tel: 3760

Sri Lankan Embassy,
Muraka,
Orchid Magu. tel: 2845

Indian Embassy,
Orchid Magu. tel: 3015

Libyan People's Bureau,
Orchid Magu. tel: 3001

Emergency Services
Central Hospital,
Sosun Magu. tel: 2400

Police
Ameer Ahmed Magu. tel: 999

Government offices.
Addu Development Authority,
Dhoshimeynaa Building,
Ameer Ahmed Magu. tel: 3101

Post Office,
Cnr Marine Drive and
  Chandani Magu. tel: 2255

Customs Office,
Meynaa Building. tel: 2270

Office of the President,
Marine Drive. tel: 3440

Department of Immigration
  and Emigration,
Sosun Magu. tel: 3406

Ministry of Foreign Affairs,
Marine Drive. tel: 3400

Department of Information
  and Broadcasting,
Ghaazee Building,
Ameer Ahmed Magu. tel: 3424

Ministry of Shipping and
  Foreign Investment,
Ghaazee Building,
Ameer Ahmed Magu.

Department of Tourism,
Ghaazee Building,
Ameer Ahmed Magu. tel: 3224

Ministry of Atolls
  Administration,
Doshimeynaa Building,
Ameer Ahmed Magu. tel: 2820

Maldives Airport Authority,
Fashaana Building,
Marine Drive. tel: 2210

Libraries and bookshops
Asrafee Bookshop,
Orchid Magu. tel: 3464

Novelty Bookshop,
Fareedhee Magu. tel: 2564

MID Library,
Ameer Ahmed Magu.

National Library,
Majeedi Magu. tel: 3485

Moneychangers
American Express,
8 Marine Drive. tel: 2789

Shop No. 70,
Majeedi Magu. tel: 2110

DIK,
Chandani Magu. tel: 2411

Travel agents
Akiri,
Marine Drive. tel: 2719

Ocean Sport,
52 Marine Drive. tel: 3360

Cyprea Ltd.,
25 Marine Drive. tel: 2451

Speed Travels,
1/1 Fareedhee Magu. tel: 3069

Imad's Agency,
39/2 Chandani Magu. tel: 3441

Universal Enterprises,
15 Chandani Magu. tel: 3080

Laaba Travels,
Ostria,
Ameer Ahmed Magu,
Henveiru. tel: 3190

Quest Enterprises,
Hickory,
Henveiru. tel: 2952

Malam International,
8 Majeedi Magu,
Henveiru. tel: 3389

Safari Tours,
S.E.K. No. 1,
Chandani Magu. tel: 2516

ZSS Tours,
5 Fiyaatoshi Golhi,
Henveiru. tel: 2505

Voyages Maldives,
2 Fareedhee Magu. tel: 2019

Kaafu

Population	— 4,153 (plus Male: 29,522)
Inhabited Islands	— 10
Uninhabited Islands	— 105
Capital	— Male

Geographically Male is a mere link in a double chain of islands known traditionally as Male atoll, or more commonly as Kaafu. An agglomeration of islands and *finolhus* (sandbanks) spreads north to south for more than 100kms and only ten, including Male, are inhabited. The remainder are predominantly tourist resorts or islands reserved for official purposes.

Doonidhoo, just north of Male, is the one-time residence of the former British Governor, and still today his large coral bungalow stands alone on this small oval-shaped island. Nowadays, it is home for several outstanding political prisoners — relatives and friends of Ibrahim Nasir, the former President — purportedly exiled for life for instigating the attempted coup in the early 1980s.

Nearby is **Kuda Bandos**, a small densely vegetated island with a magnificent beach and lagoon and a small tea shop serving *sā* and sandwiches. Several foreign companies have offered astronomical amounts hoping that the government will lease the island and permit a tourist resort to be developed, but to no avail. The island is reserved for local holiday-makers. On Fridays, only locals are allowed on the island, though on other days everyone is welcome, provided they arrange their own transport and leave the island before sunset. And of course pay the nominal Rf1 entry fee on arrival.

Also close by is **Funadhoo** which once housed a coconut fibre mill and later, a poultry farm and is now reserved for government employees who man the oil storage tanks. And to the north is **Thaburudhoo** where access is also prohibited to all but approved personnel, although some *don mihun* are known to frequent the nearby reef, reputedly the best surfing spot in Kaafu.

The resort islands

Most visitors patronise the resort islands which are scattered the length and breadth of Kaafu. Some of them are a few minutes' boatride from the airport, others are at most a couple of hours, a large majority of them are bound to have a tour guide and transport waiting to meet every international flight. But if you should arrive without a reservation and the resort of your choice is not represented at the airport, head-off to Male and contact the resort office, and transport will soon be arranged. Or simply choose another resort.

Kanifinolhu is one of the most talked-about resorts. It's by no means elaborate or star-class but it suits the environment and appeals to the young and the young-at-heart. And particularly to those who *parlez Francaise*. The management claim it's *le juste milieu,* as well as offering a variety of entertainment — from paragliding to deep-sea fishing — and a superb French-style cuisine.

Farukolufushi, only 3kms from the airport, is reserved for "Club Med" members, and so too is **Thulaagiri**, a smaller, more pleasantly-designed resort about one-hour's boatride due west of the airport. As is the philosophy behind all Club Med resorts, the standard package for guests includes all meals and sports, and both these islands can lay claim to frequent lavish cosmopolitan buffets, unmatched on any other resorts.

Furana is an Australian-owned resort noted for its convenient access to the airport and Male. Because of its magnificent deep lagoon, it provides a suitable anchorage for visiting schooners and ketches, which guests of the island are able to charter. The resort is renowned for its comfortable spacious bungalows, a small gambling casino (the only one in the country) and, unfortunately, its constant supply of brackish pungent bore water. Take plenty of shampoo for washing — soap is useless!

Makunudhoo, further to the north, offers the best anchorage facilities for visiting yachts, so guests always have a good selection of boats, which they can hire for day-long or extended tours of the atoll. And although the resort is quite small, the cabanas are reasonably good and the food is fabulous.

Leisure Island, or Kana Oiy Hura as it is traditionally known, has a number of sophisticated man-made "leisures", such as air-conditioned rooms, a well-appointed discotheque and a professionally-designed tennis court. But the most outstanding feature, one that has amazed and horrified visitors to the island, is that there is no beach or lagoon. The rates are cheaper than most other resorts, and if you're looking for a night-out to dine and dance Leisure Island is worth remembering.

Meerufenfushi is the largest, easternmost island in Kaafu, and houses the biggest resort in the Maldives. There are 130 rooms ringing the island and guests would be well-advised to opt for the older-style bungalows as they are far more airy and spacious. "Meeru", with its massive wide lagoon, is ideally suited to windsurfing enthusiasts and it is conveniently situated a matter of minutes from Diffushi, one of the largest villages in Kaafu.

Gasfinolhu literally means "tree on a sandbank". And beside the 18 small cabanas that's about all it has to offer.

Hudhuveli has 40-odd cabanas running through the centre of the island and, as the name suggests, there is little more than "white sand". Indeed pencil-thin white sand, which is usually washed completely away when the tide rolls in.

Reethi Rah — the "Beautiful Island" — is known traditionally as Medhufinolhu and is no more than a long sandbank with very little vegetation, and apart from its diving school there's not much to attract one's attention. However, for those arriving during the low season, on a budget, it may be worth noting: a room and meals is reputed to cost $55 a double, and all sporting facilities are free.

Ihuru is widely regarded as the picture-postcard-pretty resort: small, oval-shaped, thickly vegetated and surrounded by a clear turquoise lagoon. According to many visitors, its greatest detraction is the somewhat bland cuisine and the equally boring dead coral reef.

Hembadhoo is among the best of the locally-owned resorts, offering not only a superb beach and lagoon but also 30-odd spacious comfortable cabanas.

Boduhithi is a popular destination for Italian travellers, which is hardly surprising given the mounds of spaghetti bolognaise and the fact that most of the staff speak almost fluent Italiano, and closeby is **Kudahithi**, a small insignificant sandbank with six cabanas, a resort which attracts those who are affluent and demand no more than solitude.

Bandos is no more than a half-hour boatride from the airport and is renowned for its Barrakuda Diving School and an internationally-trained instructor, Herwarth Voigtmann, who feeds sharks and moray eels mouth-to-mouth. But unfortunately the resort is also noted for its cold, unimaginative decor and a cafeteria-like air-conditioned restaurant. Apart from those who come for the "shark circus", the resort appeals mainly to visiting diplomats and VIPs.

Universal Enterprises, the largest local tour operator, manage several resorts around Kaafu and even a few in a neighbouring atoll, and compared to the competition they are all of a relatively high standard. **Villingili** is their most sophisticated and also their largest and most conveniently situated, about 2kms from the capital. But **Kurumba**, the first resort to be built in the Maldives, is perhaps their most popular, due largely to the fact that it serves as the local headquarters for Eurodivers, a Swiss-run diving school, one of the biggest and best in the Maldives. To the north, about an hour or more from the airport, are **Baros** and **Nakatchafushi**, and here, too, one can find all the usual Universal offerings, including a choice of deluxe-style cabanas with refrigerator and air-conditioning.

Heading south from the airport, beyond the capital and the five kilometre-wide Vaadhoo *kandu,* there is a 30km-long chain of islands known traditionally as South Male atoll.

Velassaru, in the northwest pocket of this chain, was once listed amongst the "top 300 hotels in the world" but since the recent change in management it has become widely regarded as "a last resort", and in fact the government was once forced to temporarily close the island due to the poor hygiene facilities.

Embudu is said to house one of the best coral reefs in Kaafu, a perfect destination for snorkelling enthusiasts, and the resort boasts punctual professional service and hot and cold water in each of the cabanas.

Rannalhi is about two hours' boatride from the airport and is one of the most popular resorts in Kaafu. The natural beauty of the island, good service and comfortable cabanas invariably override the single complaint voiced by all visitors: brackish water!

Cocoa Island, or Maakunufushi as locals know it, is operated by a former *Playboy* photographer. It is unique, small and very expensive. There are only twelve thatched huts, each two-tiered, fan-cooled and beautifully decorated, a small restaurant and a few faciliites for skiing, snorkelling and windsurfing. The emphasis is on simplicity and solitude, and the owner, Eric Klemm, offers a bed and excellent meals for around $50 per person, or if you wish you can rent the whole island for about $4000 a week — a tempting thought if you can afford it.

Biyaadhoo and **Villivaru** are both outstanding, and bear the similar professional stamp that is worn by every Taj hotel in Asia. Taj, the affluent Indian-owned conglomerate, which operates the Taj Mahal Hotel in Bombay and the Sumudra in Colombo, has spared no expense in developing its resort islands and providing its guests with a selection of imported cabin cruisers and launches. Biyaadhoo is a two-storey complex with air-conditioned rooms and restaurant, tanks filled with hot and cold rainwater running to every room, and even a small hydro-ponics factory to ensure there is always a selection of fresh vegetables. And Villivaru, a hop and skip to the south, though not quite as dynamic, is nonetheless professional — and cheaper, too.

The following alphabetical list of Kaafu atoll resorts indicates the office address in Male, the office and island phone numbers, telex number, single/double room rates, number of rooms and the distance from the airport.

Asdhoo Polycom Investments, Luxwood No. 2, Marine Drive. tel: 2972; tlx: 66091 Polycom. $48/64; 27 rooms; 44kms.

Bandos Deans Orchid Agency, 2/11 Marine Drive. tel: 2844, 2667; tlx: 66050 Bandos. $55/70; 105 rooms; 8kms.

Baros Universal Enterprises, No. 15 Chandani Magu. tel: 3080, 2672; tlx: 66024 Unient. $58/63; 50 rooms; 16kms.

Biyaadhoo Prabalaji Enterprises, Maagala, Henveiru. tel: 2717, 3516; tlx: 77003 Taj. $77/95; 86 rooms; 30kms.

Bodufinolhu Sea Sand Travels,Nasandhura Palace Hotel. tel: 2149, 3525; tlx: 66041 Seasand. $40/45; 22 rooms, 39kms.

Boduhithi Safari Tours, S.E.K. No. 1, Chandani Magu. tel: 2516, 3198; tlx: 66030 Safari. $75/90; 61 rooms; 29kms.

Bolifushi Gemini Tours, Nasandhura Palace Hotel. tel: 2835, 2517; tlx: 66071 Gemini. $50/50; 32 rooms, 13kms.

Cocoa Island Naagin, Lonuziyaarai Magu, Henveiru. tel: 2120, $50/100; 12 rooms; 19kms.

Dhigufinolhu Sanreef Ltd, 3/2 Fareedhee Magu. tel: 2357, 3599; tlx: 66067 Sanreef. $40/52; 30 rooms; 19kms.

Embudu Kaimoo Travels & Hotels Services, Roanuge, Henveiru. tel: 2212, 2673; tlx: 66035 Kaimo. $48/60; 58 rooms; 8kms.

Embudu Finolhu Crescent No. 15, Marine Drive. tel: 2134. $45/50; 10 rooms; 8kms.

Eriyadu AAA and Trading Co., 29 Chandani Magu. tel: 2540, 2636; tlx: 66031 Aribcol. $48/59; 28 rooms; 39kms.

Farukolufushi Club Mediterranee, Olympia, Ahmedi Bazaar. tel: 3341, 3021; tlx: 66057 Medmald. $65/130; 52 rooms; 3kms.

Fiha Lhohi No. 4 Orchid Magu. tel: 2903, 3118; tlx: 66065 Lhohi. $48/64; 81 rooms; 42kms.

Furana Treasure Island Enterprises, No. 8 Marine Drive. tel: 2798, 3509; tlx: 66012 Furana. $64/86; 62 rooms; 5kms.

Gasfinolhu Dhirham, Faamudheyri Magu. tel: 3369, 2078; tlx: 77050 Medmald. $55/110; 29 rooms, 18kms.

Giraavaru Snow Rose, Koarukedi Magu, Henveiru. tel: 3386. $46/55; 20 rooms; 11kms.

Helengeli No. 31 Chandani Magu. tel: 3574, 2754; tlx: 66088 Lanfin. $48/60; 24 rooms; 52kms.

Hembadhoo Journeyworld, No. 16 Marine Drive. tel: 2016; tlx: 66084 Jeworld. $50/55; 34 rooms; 39kms.

Hudhuveli Deans Orchid Agency, 2/11 Marine Drive. tel: 2844, 3396;

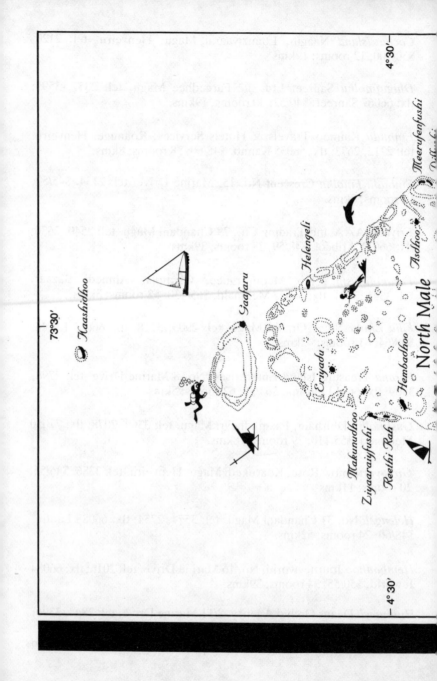

4°30'

73°30'

Haashidhoo

Gaafaru

Helengeli

Meerufenfushi

Asdhoo

Dhikuri

Eriyadu

Makunudhoo

Ziyaaraiyfushi

Reethi Rah

Hembadhoo

North Male

4°30'

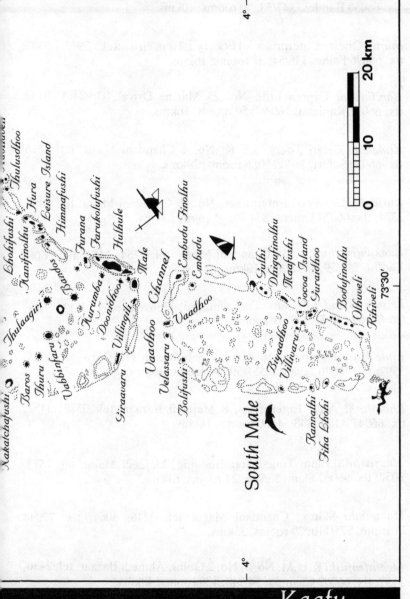

Kaafu

South Male

Nakatchafushi
Baros
Thulaagiri
Thuru
Vabbinfaru
Giraavaru
Chohifushi
Kanifinolhu
Bandos
Kurumba
Doonidhoo
Villingili
Velassaru
Vaadhoo
Bolifushi
Hura
Leisure Island
Himmafushi
Furana
Farukolufushi
Male
Hulhule
Hulhule
Vaadhoo Channel
Embudu
Embudu Finolhu
Gulhi
Rannalhi
Fiha Lhohi
Biyaadhoo
Villivaru
Dhigufinolhu
Maafushi
Cocoa Island
Guraidhoo
Bodufinolhu
Olhuveli
Rihiveli
Thulasdhoo

4°

4°

73°30'

0   10   20 km

tlx: 66050 Bandos. $47/58; 40 rooms; 10kms.

Ihuru Quest Enterprises, Hickory, Henveiru. tel: 2952, 3502; tlx: 66096 Faihu. $48/54; 37 rooms; 16kms.

Kanifinolhu Cyprea Ltd., No. 25 Marine Drive. tel: 2451, 3152; tlx: 66072 Kanimat. $60/92; 50 rooms; 16kms.

Kudahithi Safari Tours, S.E.K. No. 1 Chandani Magu. tel: 2516; tlx: 66030 Safari. $100/150; 6 rooms; 29kms.

Kurumba Universal Enterprises, No. 15 Chandani Magu. tel: 3080, 2324; tlx: 66024 Unient. $54/70; 65 rooms; 3kms.

Lankanfinolhu No. 31 Chandani Magu. tel: 2754, 3156; tlx: 66088 Lanfin. $48/59; 45 rooms; 10kms.

Leisure Island Lil Club, Thoraamaage, Henveiru. tel: 3613, 3088; tlx: 66069 Lil. $55/70; 10 rooms; 16kms.

Little Hura Garabuge, 16 Abadah Fehi Magu, Henveiru. tel: 2335, 3592; tlx: 66076 Jayatun. $51/59; 34 rooms; 16kms.

Lhohifushi Altaf Enterprises, 8 Majeedi Bazaar. tel: 3378, 3451; tlx: 66047 Altaf. $43/54; 60 rooms; 18kms.

Maayaafushi Slam Tours, Star Building, Majeedi Magu. tel: 2513, 3032; tlx: 66067 Slam. $36/46; 24 rooms; 61kms.

Makunudu Skitex, Chandani Magu. tel: 3246, 3064; tlx: 77044 Fortune. $75/110; 29 rooms; 35kms.

Meerufenfushi K.U.M. No. 5, No. 2 Golhi, Ahmedi Bazaar. tel: 2430, 3157; tlx: 66002 Champa. $47/48; 130 rooms; 40kms.

Nakatchafushi Universal Enterprises, No. 15 Chandani Magu. tel: 3080, 2665; tlx: 66024 Unient. $58/63; 43 rooms, 23kms.

Olhuveli Laaba Travels, Ostria, Ameer Ahmed Magu, Henveiru. tel: 3190, 2788; tlx: 66064 Laaba. $48/60; 50 rooms, 39kms.

Rannalhi Jetan Travel, No. 55 Marine Drive. tel: 3323, 2688; tlx: 66086 Jetan. $48/58, 51 rooms, 44kms.

Reethi Rah No. 29 Marine Drive. tel: 2726, 2077; tlx: 77046 Rerare. $55/90; 50 rooms; 35kms.

Rihiveli Dhaharaage, No. 1 Chandani Magu. tel: 3767, 3731; tlx: 66072. $43/48; 36 rooms; 40 kms.

Thulaagiri Club Mediterranee, Olympia, Ahmedi Bazaar. tel: 2816; tlx: 66053 Thula. $63/126; 29 rooms; 11kms.

Vaadhoo Reef Side, Orchid Magu. tel: 3545. 3397; tlx: 66025 Reef. $40/60; 16 rooms; 8kms.

Vabbinfaru No. 8 Marine Drive. tel: 2537, 3147; tlx: 77026 Vabbin. $48/59; 25 rooms; 16kms.

Velassaru Sea Sand Travels, Nasandhura Palace Hotel. tel: 3380, 3041; tlx: 66041 Seasand $40/45; 45 rooms; 10kms.

Villingili Universal Enterprises, No. 15 Chandani Magu. tel: 3080, 2154; tlx: 66024 Unient. $54/59; 113 rooms, 3kms.

Villivaru Prabalaji Enterprises, Maagala, Henveiru. tel: 2717, 3598; tlx: 77003 Taj. $63/80; 60 rooms; 29kms.

Ziyaaraiyfushi No. 18 Orchid Magu. tel: 3088; tlx: 77008 Ominex. $30/35; 29 rooms; 34kms.

The fishing villages

According to the travel brochures, the villages around Kaafu atoll — excluding Male — are "typical Maldivian fishing villages". True or false, one thing is certain — these villages have definitely reaped the rewards of being in close proximity to the major tourist traffic.

Almost every day these nine so-called "fishing villages" are visited by a boatload of tourists who arrive from the nearby resorts to do a quick tour of an inhabited island, bargain with the locals over the price of valuable or worthless shells and home-made jewellery, and perhaps even enjoy a game of soccer or volleyball with the local kids. Here, unlike the far-flung villages, the inhabitants no longer look upon *don mihun* with fear and suspicion, in fact you are widely regarded as an important ingredient in the island's economy. The traditional occupations, fishing and weaving, no longer hold pride of place in these villages, because it is much easier and more profitable to sit at home and make and sell local souvenirs. And even the local *fihara* (shop) has expanded its shelves from the simple lines of rice, flour, sugar and spices to include boxes of Colgate toothpaste, canned foods and biscuits to satisfy the *don mihun's* needs for a few home comforts.

For those who are keen to taste the local lifestyle — albeit somewhat tainted by tourism — Kaafu is an ideal destination, particularly if your travel time is restricted.

Himmafushi is the closest fishing village to Male, about an hour by an engine-propelled *dorni* or two hours by sail. It is large and densely vegetated, houses less than 400 people and most of them are involved, one way or another, in the small local tourist industry. The arriving visitor is confronted by a long row of small thatched "tourist shops", signboards in misspelt German, Italian, French and English, and even a couple of tea shops, a rare sight indeed in the far-flung villages.

Hura is a few kilometres north of Himmafushi and a far cry from its heyday when it was the home of Hassan Izzaddeen, a popular 18th century Sultan. Today the *kateeb* and his family are renowned through Kaafu for enjoying great wealth and influence, and not only do they boast the largest tourist shop and the only tea shop on Hura, but also own the biggest and best *dorni* and a small electric generator used to provide current to the homes of their friends and relatives.

Thulusdhoo is about three hours' cruising from Male and many locals will tell you it's the most beautiful village in Kaafu, ringed by many isolated sandy coves, and close by is a long deserted island where you can perhaps spend the day — alone. Traders from the neighbouring atolls, Raa and Baa, often sail across for the day to sell their *lonu mas* (salted fish) at the government warehouse on the outskirts of Thulus-dhoo.

Diffushi is one of a half-dozen islands lying in the wide expanse of shallow turquoise water which spreads for several kilometres across the eastern fringe of Kaafu. The village, 500-strong, is renowned first and foremost for its fishing, and in the late afternoon you will usually find one or two 20 metre-long engine *dornis* bound from Diffushi to Male, ladened with tonnes of tuna. And during the high tourist season you will often see the youngsters on the nearby reef plucking lobsters from the caverns and selling them to tourists — Rf20 will get you a good size lobster.

Gaafaru borrows its name from and sits alone on the longest reef in the Maldives — 10kms long and 8kms wide — so it should not surprise that the island is a popular destination with diving enthusiasts, particularly as the reef has become a graveyard for dozens of cargo ships.

Kaashidhoo with nearly 1000 inhabitants, is the largest village (beyond Male) in Kaafu. It lies isolated at the centre of the infamous Kaashidhoo *kandu*, nearly 25kms from the nearest island and six hour's cruising from Male. The village is renowned nationwide as the best place to buy *dia hakuru* (coconut honey) and a good place to anchor overnight for any *dorni* bound to or from the northern atolls.

Gulhi is a small picture-postcard-pretty island about 20kms — or two hours' cruising — south of Male, and it houses less than 300 people. It is extremely popular with travellers.

Maafushi is a long and narrow island, a little further south of Gulhi. Its most outstanding aspect is the segregated reformatory school for orphans and young wayward children, and a government warehouse that buys *lonu mas* from traders in the nearby atolls. Almost any day of the week, you can be reasonably sure to see a *dorni* arriving from Alifu or Laamu atoll, the crew unload and sell their bundles of salted fish and immediately set-off back home.

Guraidhoo is a far cry from its heyday when it served as a holiday resort for locals. Nowadays it boasts a community of 400 people, a few of whom suffer from leprosy.

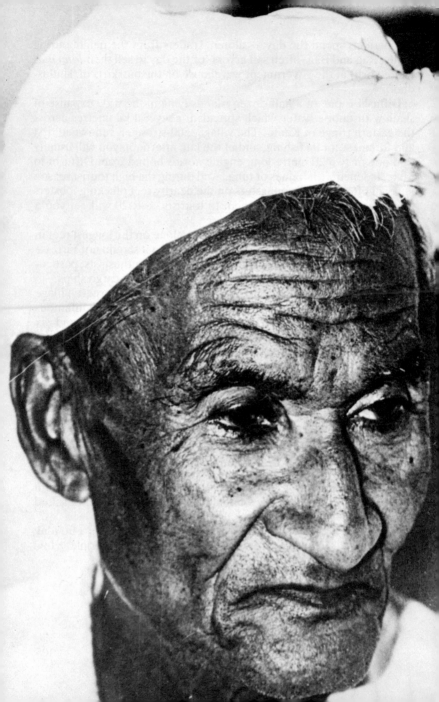

To the outer atolls

If you truly want to get away from it all, set your sights beyond Kaafu atoll where you will soon discover a myriad unique villages, deserted islands, unpolluted water, abundant sea life and even some quite outstanding resorts.

If you've the time and the money to spare, a popular course is to hire a registered vessel and plan your own island-hopping itinerary. Consult the travel agents in Male. It matters little whether you travel north, south or wander around the central atolls, for newcomers the islands are all much the same.

Wherever you go, however, be prepared for the "welcome" when you visit the farther-flung villages. You may well be the first *don miha* they have ever seen, so the women will flee, the children will scream and the men will stare, curiously, from a distance. But then again they soon become bolder and before long you will find yourself engulfed by interested onlookers, prodding and questioning, annoying and delighting. They are a fun-loving, promiscuous, non-violent race of people — you'll see or hear no more than a loud verbal argument — and when you remember that many of these islanders have not once left their shore, you'll appreciate the innocence of a question like: *handu onaani kalemeng rashuga?* — does the moon shine on your island?

Day in, day out, in every village you'll find something to interest you. On the beach you may find the local *fandita* man practising his ritual onboard a new boat, to bless it with luck before launching. And elsewhere there may be preparations for a *kaveni sā* for a newly-married couple, or a *maalud* for a young boy who has been circumcised. Or you may well see, and become involved in, the local *raiatung,* when everyone congregates to perform a community service, such as sweeping the streets or building a new wharf.

While you're here in these isolated villages a simple gift, like a tin of condensed milk (the islanders love it in their tea), is very much appreciated and moreover might even earn you passage on a day-long fishing trip, on which you could easily score a boatload of tuna. Of course you could also choose to camp overnight on a deserted island and there are plenty to choose from. You'll usually find a fresh-water well, which is fine for cooking and drinking, and there may even be a small thatched hut which is suitable for a short-term shelter. Sometimes there may even be a *raaveri* and his son who live on the island, to collect the *raa* from the trees, and they'll always offer you some of this deliciously sweet and refreshing nectar. But if you're tempted to stay a few days, don't forget to stock up on basic essentials like rice, flour, sugar, spices, salt, fruit and vegetables, kerosene for the *fulibati* and a good knife for cutting fish and collecting firewood. You can buy these things from a nearby inhabited island, or there's a wide variety of useful bits-and-pieces around the Ahmedi Bazaar in Male.

And if you choose to simply dream about such adventures, look towards the resort islands a day away from Kaafu, or deep down in the south — life beyond Kaafu is closer to the heart of the Maldives.

108

Alifu

Population	—	6,223
Inhabited Islands	—	18
Uninhabited Islands	—	61
Capital	—	Mahibadhoo

Sailing due west of Male, across the 40km-wide Ariadhoo *kandu,*
brings you to a small group of islands and *finolhus* known traditionally
as Rasdu atoll. About ten kilometres distant, to the north, is **Thoddoo**,
large, isolated and renowned for its ancient Buddhist temple — or at
least the remains of one — and a vineyard of huge watermelons. And
southwest of here is Ari, the archetypal atoll, a perfect chain of islands
extending 80kms from north to south and 30kms across. For hundreds
of years, the people here were skilled at catching turtles from the ocean
and weaving sails out of palm leaves, but nowadays the inhabitants are
more noted for their fishing and carpentry skills and for their small cot-
tage industry — their sculptors specialise in coral tombstones.

Fenfushi, in particular, is famous for its coral carvings and a number
of ancient mosques, renovated many times. Enroute through the atoll
stop off at **Hurasdhoo**, an uninhabited island noted for its pineapples
before a month-long fire destroyed the island's vegetation.

The region embracing Rasdu, Thoddoo and Ari — popularly known
as Alifu — is an easily-accessible retreat for anyone who cares to
escape the well-worn tourist tracks around Kaafu and, fortunately, the
government has recognised the obvious benefits of planning its tourist
program, insisting on a limit to the number of resorts in Alifu and
thereby ensuring that the villages remain — as far as possible — whole-
somely traditional.

Nonetheless there are a couple of outstanding places to stay and the
two to six hour voyage can be made direct from the airport if you book
in advance at one of the resorts. Or if you prefer to hitch, look around
Male harbour for the peculiar junk-like *dornis* marked with an "I".
They are unique, and bound for Alifu. A lift should cost around Rf30
— if you bargain well!

109

The resort islands

Kuramathi is the first island one sights enroute west from Male, after three hours' cruising across the Ariadhoo *kandu*. It's a popular route with diving enthusiasts travelling on a healthy budget, since the facilities on the island are typical of the comfortable resorts operated by Universal Enterprises. A nearby reef is home to a school of hammerhead sharks.

Sailing further west, an hour or so, brings you to a small picturesque island called Kuda Foludhoo. Hidden beyond the dense vegetation is the **Nika Hotel**, a million-dollar resort, the most original and outstanding resort in the Maldives. Just a few of the special attractions include the air-conditioned launch that ferries you from the airport in under two hours and the choice of fifteen spacious, artistic, conical cabanas with hot and cold desalinised water on tap. And there's a selection of restaurants — one on the shore, another on the fringing reef and yet another, with a huge wine-cellar, underground. And for the staff, a mosque; not just any corrugated iron-clad mosque, but a beautiful dome-shaped construction to meld in with the ambience. The entire concept is the brain-child of an Italian architect whose dream was to construct a village where those with money could enjoy their individual fantasies. But a note of caution: book well in advance.

Towards the centre of the atoll, you'll find a further selection of resort islands, none to compare with the Nika, but well worth a visit if you're looking at comfort and less cost. A few relevant details about the resorts around Alifu includes the following:

Bathala Treasure Island Enterprises, No. 8 Marine Drive. tel: 2798; tlx: 66012 Furana. $55/65; 17 rooms; 53kms.

Dhiggiri Safari Tours, S.E.K. No. 1 Chandani Magu. tel: 2516, 3592; tlx: 66030 Safari. $55/65; 30 rooms; 60kms.

Fesdhoo Universal Enterprises, No. 15 Chandani Magu. tel: 3080, 3741; tlx: 66024 Unient. $55/60; 45 rooms; 65kms.

Halaveli Akiri, Marine Drive. tel: 2719, 2592; tlx: 66022 Engeli. $30/50; 20 rooms; 55kms.

Kuramathi Universal Enterprises, No. 15 Chandani Magu. tel: 3080, 2456; tlx: 66024 Unient. $58/63; 100 rooms; 58kms.

Nika Hotel No. 5 Orchid Magu. tel:2881; tlx: 77024 Nika. $65/130; 15 rooms; 69kms.

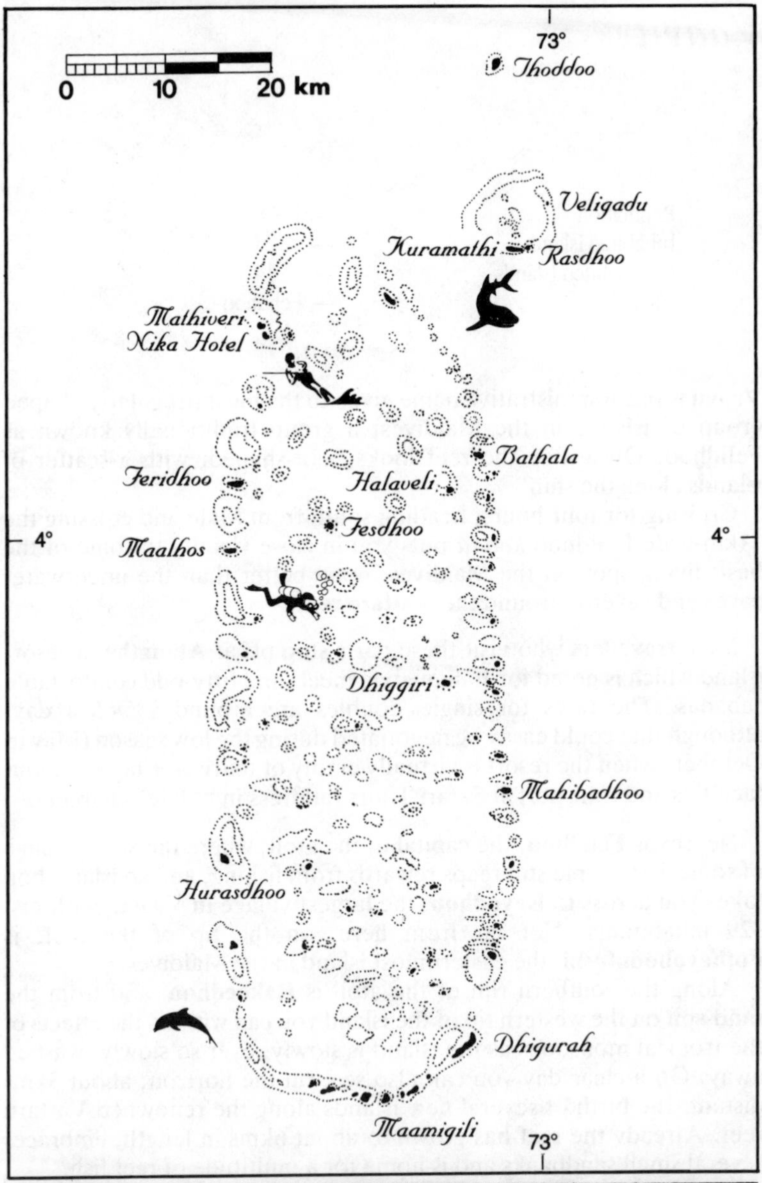

Thoddoo

73°

Veligadu

Kuramathi

Rasdhoo

Mathiveri
Nika Hotel

Bathala

Feridhoo

Halaveli

Fesdhoo

4°

Maalhos

4°

Dhiggiri

Mahibadhoo

Hurasdhoo

Dhigurah

Maamigili

73°

Alifu

Vaavu

Population	— 1,078
Inhabited Islands	— 5
Uninhabited Islands	— 14
Capital	— Felidhoo

Vaavu is the administrative name given to the most irregularly-shaped group of islands in the Maldives, a group traditionally known as Felidhoo. On a map the reef looks boot-shaped, with a scatter of islands along the shin.

Cruising for four hours, heading south from Male and crossing the 11km-wide Fulidhoo *kandu* puts you in close vicinity to some of the best diving spots in the Maldives, none better than the underwater caves and caverns around the **Vattaru reef.**

Most travellers who visit these parts stop off at **Alimatha**, a resort island which is noted for Italian-style meals and fifty-odd comfortable cabanas. The rates for singles/doubles are around $55/65 a day, although that could easily be negotiated during the low season (May to October) when the resort is virtually empty of tourists. Enquire about facilities and transport at Safari Tours (address in "Male" chapter).

Nearby is **Felidhoo**, the capital of the atoll, where the small village of some 300 people still reaps rewards from fishing, and an island-hop takes you across to **Keyodhoo**, the largest village in Vaavu, with just 329 inhabitants. Not far from here, on the tip of the reef, is **Fotheyobodufushi**, the easternmost island in the Maldives.

Along the southern rim of the atoll is **Rakeedhoo**, and from the sand-spit on the western tip of the island you can witness the effects of the tropical monsoons as the island is slowly, ever so slowly, washed away. On a clear day you can also see, on the horizon, about 3kms distant, the birth of several new islands along the renowned Vattaru reef. Already the reef has grown to about 6kms in length, embraces several small sandbanks and is home for a multitude of reef fish.

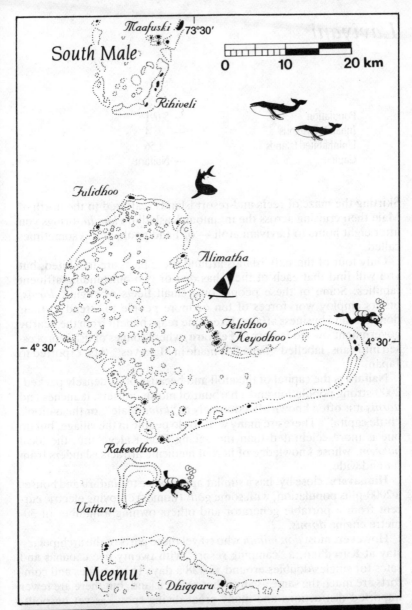

South Male

Maafuski 73°30'

0   10   20 km

Rihiveli

Fulidhoo

Alimatha

Felidhoo
Keyodhoo

— 4° 30'   4° 30' —

Rakeedhoo

Vattaru

Meemu

Dhiggaru

Vaavu

Laviyani

Population	— 5,691
Inhabited Islands	— 4
Uninhabited Islands	— 56
Capital	— Naifaru

Skirting the maze of reefs and resort islands scattered to the north of Male then cruising across the infamous Kashidhoo *kandu*, brings you after eight hours to Laviyani atoll — or Faadippolu as it is sometimes called.

Only four of the sixty islands around these parts are inhabited, but you will find that each of them has one or two outstanding affluent families. Some of these people own small fleets of engine *dornis*, others employ workforces of ten or more people to attend to their domestic and business affairs. Everyone reaps benefit from the nearby government-owned factory at **Felivaru**, where tonnes of fish is processed into cans, labelled "Tuna fish made in Maldives", then exported to Japan.

Naifaru is the capital of the atoll and because of its densely packed, 2000-strong population and a harbour of motor cruisers, launches and *dornis* it is often known affectionately as "*kuda* Male", or the nation's "little capital". There are many well-to-do people in the village, but no one is more celebrated than the ageing Don Kalegefanu, the local *hakeem*, whose knowledge of herbal medicine attracts islanders from far and wide.

Hinnavaru, close by, has a similar appearance to Naifaru and houses a 2000-plus population, with some *gotis* (homes) enjoying electric current from a portable generator and others owning a number of 30-metre engine *dornis*.

However, most *don mihun* who travel these parts of the archipelago stay at **Kuredhoo**, a "camping resort" with twenty-five cabanas and rates for singles/doubles around $28/38 a day. The facilities and comforts are much the same as any other resort island, but there are fewer imported distractions and many great diving spots, as yet unspoilt.

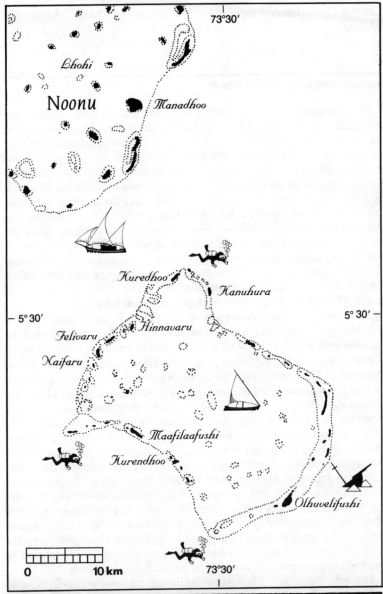

Lhohi

Noonu

Manadhoo

Kuredhoo

Kanuhura

— 5° 30′

5° 30′ —

Felivaru

Hinnavaru

Naifaru

Maafilaafushi

Kurendhoo

Olhuvelifushi

73°30′

0   10 km

73°30′

Laviyani

Contact Quest Enterprises for further details (see "Male" chapter for address).

Bonito Fishing in the Maldive Islands

The bonito season is harvest-time for the Maldivians; the period of prosperity and greatest activity. Special boats are built for the bonito fishing, long, beamy, graceful craft, fine of line and of shallow draught as befits vessels that have their home in coral-infested lagoons of little depth. As seen at Minicoy, the hull is stoutly built, open except for a short decking at each end, and is divided into a number of compartments by means of six or seven cross-partitions or bulkheads. The prow rises high, curving gracefully upwards into a tall, snake-like stemhead not unlike that of an old Viking ship which, indeed, the boat as a whole closely resembles. The after-decking extends outwards over the quarters into a wide platform, shaped like the expanded wings of a butterfly; from this the actual fishing takes place. A single pole mast is placed fairly well forward; as in many of our own fishing boats, instead of being stepped permanently in position, the butt end is pivoted between two uprights, the "tabernacle" as it is named by sailors; this permits of it being lowered at will, when it rests in the crutch of a short upright post fitted near the stern. The rig is a strange combination of fore-and-aft and squaresails. A high rectangular mat sail, the head laced to a yard, is hoisted on the fore side of the mast, while abaft, on the same spar, is set a fore-and-aft mainsail, laced to a gaff, but without a boom.

Before setting out for the fishing grounds small fishes for use as live bait have to be collected. These are caught in the lagoon in a baited square of netting extended on four poles, one attached to each corner, put out from the side of a boat. The outer margin is lowered under the water and ground bait scattered over the surface. When the small fishes have gathered to the feast, the net is suddenly lifted and the fishes taken out. The catch consists of two principal sorts, a small fish like a minnow and a larger one about the size of a sardine. Until required, they are imprisoned in substantially constructed wicker cages, some five and a half feet long by about three feet across and about three and a half feet deep. The mouth is left open until the fishes are put in, when a net is spread over it, to prevent sea-birds from gormandizing on the contents at their leisure. Each cage is anchored out in the lagoon, buoyed up by two stout baulks of light wood, one on either side. In Japan, where parallel methods of bonito fishing are practised, the live-bait cage is a huge globular basket, floated by two stout bamboos. In this manner small fishes are often kept alive for five or six days, awaiting the advent of favourable fishing conditions.

To accommodate the live bait aboard the fishing boat, two compartments are fitted up as live wells, one immediately forward of the mast, the other just abaft it. Each has from four to six plugged holes in the bottom. Just before sailing a supply of live bait is transferred to these two wells and the holes are unplugged so that continuous streams of water spout inwards. This inrush of water would speedily swamp the boat were it not that two men are set to work to keep pace with it by bailing. By means of perforations at suitable and varying heights in the intervening bulkheads the inflowing water is conducted to the aftermost compartment where the two bailers stand. In this way the water in the wells is maintained in a fit condition to keep alive the stock of little fishes.

Each boat carries a large crew all equipped with short rods save the steersman, the two bailers, four splashers and three or four boys to manage the big mat sail. Each rod is a bamboo about six feet long with a line of the same length armed with a barbless steel hook, brightly silvered, the shank broad and flat and curved to resemble as near as possible the shape of a small fish.

Once a shoal is sighted all available hands seize their rods and crowd upon the after-platforms. One of the bailers ceases work and takes up a position just aft of the mast. Here he begins to sling live bait overboard as fast as he can, dipping them up from the wells in twos and threes with a little saucer-shaped hoop net, seven or eight inches across. At the same time two men crouching on either side of the stern platform splash water with all their might, using long-handled scoops made from the flower spathe of the coconut, partly cut down and tied to one end of a light wooden handle. This is a measure of economy; the bonito has to be gulled into the belief that a large shoal of small fish is about and, without the splashing, the amount of live bait thrown out would be insufficient to carry though the deception successfully. The combination of this splashing and fall of a few fishes into the sea every few seconds, is enough to bring the hungry bonito dashing toward the boat. The men become as excited as the fish; flogging the water with their lines they dash the hooks wildly among the rushing fish. In their blind eagerness, the bonito takes live bait or hook indiscriminately. Those that make the wrong choice find themselves suddenly lifted out of the water and swung aboard at the end of a line.

While the bonito is biting freely and shoals are abundant, the catch of each man averages one a minute; two or three hours are sufficient time in which to load up the boat with a catch of six hundred or even a thousand fish.

By James Hornell.
(Late Director of Fisheries to the Government of Madras.)

Baa and Raa

Cruising twelve to thirteen hours northwest of Male takes you to a bank of islands which are famed for their exiled inhabitants, handicraftsmen and carpenters. One hundred and eighty-one islands are grouped, traditionally, into four parts: Powell's Islands, north and south Malosmadulu, and Goifufehendhoo. Or for administrative purposes they are grouped into two and called, more simply, Baa and Raa.

Baa

Population	— 5,765
Inhabited Islands	— 13
Uninhabited Islands	— 68
Capital	— Eydhafushi

Moving nor'west across the Kaashidhoo *kandu* seemingly leads nowhere, but just beyond the horizon are a few isolated sandbanks and villages — **Goidhoo**, **Fulhadhoo** and **Fehendhoo** — where many criminals spend their days in exile. This is where Francois Pyrard, the 17th century castaway, spent his first few days in the Maldives. A current resident on these islands is a German traveller, banished for life for stabbing his girlfriend to death in a small guesthouse in Male, in 1976. The story received wide international publicity, but despite his option to be transferred to a German prison, he chose to be exiled to Fulhadhoo, and now he is married and has a *darifalu* (child). And goes fishing and island-hopping as he pleases!

North of here, beyond a 10-km wide channel, is the main bank of Baa atoll, a 40km-long chain of islands known locally as Malosmadulu *dekunu buri* (southern part).

Thulaadhoo is hidden in the southwest pocket of this chain and should not be missed, for it shelters the nation's best *laielaa jehang mihun*. Every day you will find dozens of men hand-carving large and small wooden boxes, coating them with strands of red, black and yel-

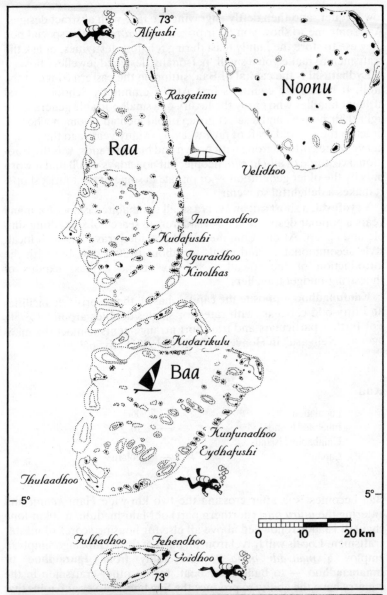

Baa and Raa

low lacquer, and then deftly engraving the face with abstract designs. Ask someone to show you their prized *maalud foshi,* the special box they use to store the family feast during religious festivities, or ask the craftsmen to make you a small, personally-designed jewellery box.

Eydhafushi is the capital of Baa, sitting on the eastern fringe of the atoll. It boasts the country's first Atoll Community School, several affluent families who enjoy the luxury of a small portable generator to light their homes, and a select group of old men and women who still practise the age-old craft of *feyli* weaving. Many years ago the *feyli,* a heavy white cotton sarong with brown and black strands, was the traditional costume of all *Divehin* people, but nowadays you'll find it worn only by the older generation — or on sale in some of the tourist shops. It makes a delightful souvenir.

Veyofushi, a short sail away, is a small uninhabited island, for many years a popular destination for wanderers in search of something simple and cheap. At one time the island provided travellers with local-style accommodation and meals for about Rf20 a day, but with the introduction of the so-called "$3 tax" came a mass exodus of shoestring-budget travellers.

Kunfunadhoo, opposite the capital, has all the resort-style facilities and fifty-odd cabanas, with rates for singles/doubles around $45/50. For further particulars and transport arrangements contact the manager at "Nelivaru" in Henveiru, Male (tel: 3256; tlx: 66009 CW).

Raa

Population	— 7,906
Inhabited Islands	— 16
Uninhabited Islands	— 74
Capital	— Ugoofaru

Baa becomes Raa after crossing the two km-wide Hani *kandu* and entering the *uturu buri* (northern part) of Malosmadulu, a 60km-long chain of islands renowned above all else for housing scores of master craftsmen. Locals will travel from all parts of the archipelago simply to employ a *maavadi miha* — preferably from **Iguraidhoo** or **Innamaadhoo** — to build their boat, for no other craftsmen in the country have the ability to produce the fine lines, curves and joins that

distinguish a *dorni* built in Raa atoll from all others.

From either of these islands it's only a short hop to **Kinholas**, where the famous 14th century Arab traveller, Ibn Battuta, once stayed, and a skip and jump to **Rasgetimu**, the original "King's Island", where Koimala Kalo first lived when he arrived nearly 2,000 years ago.

And if you're looking for an isolated retreat, a visit to **Kudafushi** is a must. There's a single tumbledown coral house in which you can camp overnight, a fresh-water well and a school of young sharks basking in the lagoon. For an unknown reason the small community of people who thrived here was moved to neighbouring islands, on April 18, 1946.

The northern atolls

Mind-boggling, tongue twisting names like Miladunmadulu, Tiladun-mati and Ihavandippolu define the northernmost atolls in the Mal-dives, but for practical purposes the 209 islands in this region are grouped into four and called Noonu, Shaviyani, Haa Dhaalu and Haa Alifu. Many visitors will swear that this is the best, most awe-inspiring destination in the Maldives, this is where island-hopping, diving and simple lifestyles are supreme, but those who live here may tell you the other, not-so-pleasant side of life on a tropical island. Here in the north, life is very much dependent on the whim of nature, everyone lives at the mercy of the Indian Ocean, and calm sea breezes can turn overnight into thunderstorms, roofs will be uplifted, trees uprooted, and some villages have been known to be rocked by a series of mild earthquakes. For the sake of survival, the northerners are far more inter-dependent than islanders in the south, and they frequently criss-cross from island to island and atoll to atoll to trade wares with their neighbours. And here, again so unlike the south, the outer rim of the atoll is frequently broken by deep narrow channels, which allow most small *dornis* to pass unheeded in and out of the atoll. The smooth-flowing ocean current ensures a luxuriant growth of coral around the majority of islands.

Noonu

Population	— 6,282
Inhabited Islands	— 14
Uninhabited Islands	— 64
Capital	— Manadhoo

The northern atolls are comprised largely of a single chain of islands, 140kms long. Noonu includes the islands in the southern part of this chain and according to many visitors and local traders no part of the archipelago is quite as beautiful. A series of reefs, an agglomeration of islands and a kaleidoscopic marine life spreads far and wide, and as testimony to its obvious attractions the government has earmarked the atoll for official tourist development, with a domestic airport now under construction on one of the deserted islands.

If you are at all historically inclined, take a day-tour to **Landu** and the uninhabited **Lhohi**, where you'll find a couple of *us fas gandus*, which supposedly confirm that an ancient Buddhist culture once thrived in these parts.

Shaviyani

Population	— 6,362
Inhabited Islands	— 15
Uninhabited Islands	— 39
Capital	— Farukolufunadhoo

Beyond the imaginary border that marks the end of Noonu and the beginning of Shaviyani, the islands become remarkably more fertile, in fact more fertile than most other islands in the northern atolls.

The capital of the atoll, **Farukolufunadhoo** — known affectionately as Funadhoo — is an ideal base from which to begin one's tour of Shaviyani. It is long, luxuriously vegetated, sparsely populated and engulfed in a wide, deep turquoise lagoon which provides perfect anchorage for the many *dornis* enroute north and south to and from Male.

Someone in the village will probably rent his sail *dorni* for a reasonable fare, and with a good wind you can hop across in less than a half-hour to **Liamagu**, the one-time capital, where the locals grow limes and bamboo, then across to **Firambadhoo**, where *goti* after *goti* grows an array of fruits and vegetables and the *bodu miha* ("big man") runs regular trips to Male with a boatful of lobsters for the tourist resorts. And then sail on to **Maaugoodoo** and up to **Feevah** where groves of sugar cane can be found, thence over to **Bilefahi**, the most picturesque village in the atoll, renowned for its many skilful women who weave *saantis* from a locally-grown reed. You can buy one of these two metre, cream coloured mats for as little as Rf5.

Before leaving the atoll it is also worthwhile arranging a trip to **Kanbalifaru**, a deserted island that is used by locals to grow *bimbi* (finger millet) and *kudi-bai* (Italian foxtail millet) and where you may

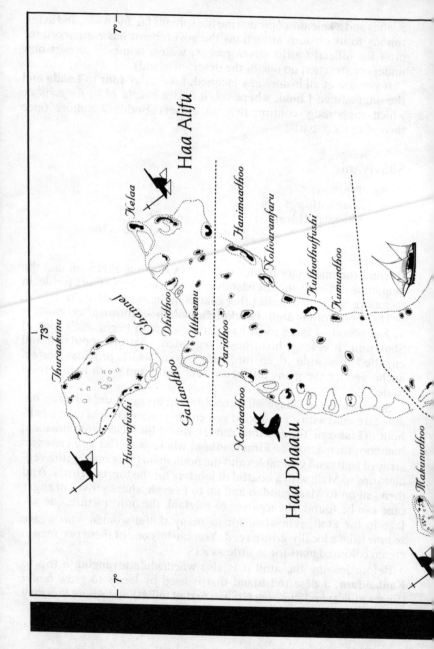

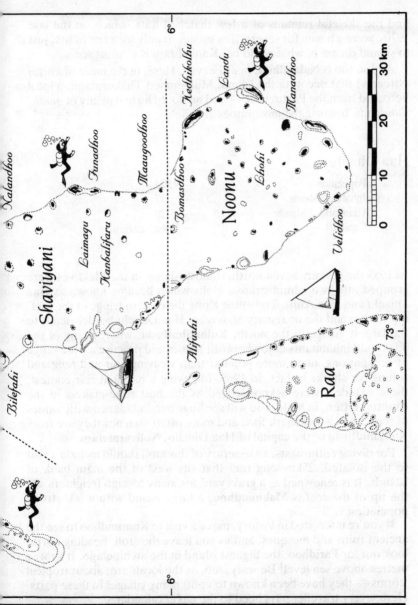

Northern atolls

find the skeletal remains of a few thatched huts, which, in the late 1970s, were a haven for several *don mihun*. If only for a few hours, just to sit and dream of what could be, Kanbalifaru is a "must see".

And so too is **Nalandhoo**, near Feevah. Here, in the maze of *korlus* (streams) that decorate the island, Muhammed Thakurufanu, a local hero, hid from the Portuguese — and no doubt he had plenty of *madiri dundandi,* because the mosquitoes are rife!

Haa Dhaalu

Population	— 9,924
Inhabited Islands	— 17
Uninhabited Islands	— 20
Capital	— Nolivaramfaru

In 1958 the seventy-seven northernmost islands in the Maldives were grouped into two administrative atolls which became known as Haa Dhaalu and Haa Alifu. Travelling along the eastern fringe of the reef, not far beyond the imaginary Shaviyani-Haa Dhaalu border, leads to the largest village in the north, **Kulhudhuffushi**, where many of the 3,000-odd inhabitants enjoy *borki*-lit homes and practise a wide range of occupations, none more popular than weaving coir and *fang* and fishing for shark. In fact, in 1965, following a national coir contest, these islanders were acknowledged as the best rope-makers in the country. Often, in Male, you will see huge *batelis* ladened with tonnes of rope, thatch and shark fins, and more often than not they are from Kulhuhuffushi or the capital of Haa Dhaalu, **Nolivaramfaru**.

For diving enthusiasts, an itinerary of this atoll should include a visit to the isolated, 25km-long reef that sits west of the main bank of islands. It is renowned as a graveyard for many foreign freighters. At the tip of the reef is **Makunudhoo**, a large island with a 600-strong population.

If you're interested in history, make a visit to **Kumundhoo** to see the ancient ruins and mosques, and as you leave the atoll, heading north, look out for **Faridhoo**, the highest island in the archipelago. It's three metres above sea level! Be wary, too, as the locals are, about tropical storms — they have been known to uplift many villages in these parts. Here, every traveller pays heed to the *nakai* calendar.

Haa Alifu

Population	— 8,603
Inhabited Islands	— 16
Uninhabited Islands	— 24
Capital	— Dhidhoo

Historically and culturally Haa Alifu is outstanding. Every year, in **Utheemu**, the President and several of his ministers congregate with the 330-odd inhabitants to celebrate Independence Day and pay homage at the birthplace of their saviour, Muhammed Thakurufanu. And still today Thakurufanu's home is periodically renovated as a mark of respect for his unmatched leadership in the late 16th century.

Kelaa, on the northeastern protruding tip of Tiladunmati, lays similar claim to some highly respected former inhabitants, notably their island *kateebs* who once played an important role in the Sultan's coronation. During the 1939-45 war, the island also boasted a major Indian Ocean air base, operated by the British. Nowadays, however, Kelaa's singular attraction is its abundance of yams.

Tacking nor'west from here, across the Gallandhoo *kandu,* brings you to the final chain of islands in the Maldives, the 20km-long chain known traditionally as Ihavandippolu. On the western fringe is the former atoll capital, **Huvarafushi**, famed for its *bandia jehang* and sporting prowess.

And still further north is **Thuraakunu**, the nation's northernmost island — 290kms from Minicoy, the southern part of the Indian state of Lakshadweep, where the people still speak *Divehi* and wear the traditional *Divehi hedung*.

MALDIVES
Watery Claims
India Today, October 15, 1982

Its tourist brochures carry the catchy line: "Where paradise doesn't cost the earth". For once, there is really very little advertising hype in that statement. Maldives, that tiny Indian Ocean archipelago (area: 298 sq miles; pop: 168,000) has barely begun to emerge from its cocoon of protracted isolation, and so far, its attempts to make the world aware that it is more than just a dot on the map have been confined to prospective tourists. But for the island's President, Maumoon Abdul Gayoom, that, apparently, was not a big enough splash. On Maldivian National Day recently Gayoom laid indirect claim to the Minicoys, the coral islets that are part of Indian territory.

In fact, the spark had already been ignited by Gayoom's brother, Abdulla Hameed, the provincial affairs minister, who during his speech stated that the Minicoys were historically part of Maldives. At that point, Gayoom interrupted his brother's speech to add that in his opinion the Minicoys, north of his country's maritime boundary, were part of the Maldives. Male, the country's capital, had never witnessed such excitement since an unidentified aircraft recently buzzed the island's only airport two nights in succession before disappearing as mysteriously as it appeared.

Soured Relations: To add to the sheer effrontery of the claim was the fact that one of the VIPs present during the controversial speech was none other than Brij Kumar, India's high commissioner in Male. Kumar, however, only realised the implications much later since the speech was in Divehi, the Maldivian national language, and none of the diplomats present could understand a word. If he had understood, Kumar would hardly have applauded as enthusiastically as he did.

What followed next was vintage Keystonian as the drowsy diplomatic channels between New Delhi and Male were suddenly activated. Figuratively, Gayoom's announcement was little more than a flea-bite. But in the diplomatic sense, it was a bite all the same — of the hand that feeds one. Relations between the two countries have been extremely friendly. India was one of the first countries to set up a diplomatic mission in Male, and since then New Delhi has made a major contribution to Male's development plans, including the construction of Male's international airport by the International Airports Authority of India (IAAI).

Needless Dispute: It was in that context that Gayoom's controversial statement created more ripples than it really deserved to. The day after the speech the Maldives foreign ministry, realising the implications, hastily dispatched a letter to the Indian High Commission explaining that there was no need for misunderstanding: Maldives was not laying claim to the Minicoys. According to Indian foreign office sources, the matter would have been quietly brushed under the carpet but for the fact that the statement was widely played up by the press in neighbouring Sri Lanka, and a subsequent item in the Maldivian department of information and broadcasting's news bulletins a week later which again repeated Gayoom's statements on the Minicoys.

This galvanised India into lodging the traditional diplomatic protest and Gayoom himself later denied the reports that persistently appeared in Colombo newspapers.

What rankled most was the fact that the Colombo reports hinted that Gayoom had been instigated to make the statement by "outside forces" and that it signalled the start of a boundary dispute.

As far as the Indian foreign office is concerned, the question of a boundary dispute does not arise at all. India and the Maldives signed an official maritime boundary agreement in December, 1979 as a follow-up to an earlier 1976 agreement which gave New Delhi sovereignty and exclusive jurisdiction over the Minicoys. Further, the prospect of Male bucking New Delhi at the instigation of "outside forces" is equally incomprehensible. The only remote candidate for the honour is the Soviet Union which has made Maldives a standing offer to lease Gan island, a former Royal Air Force base at the southernmost tip of the country, for US $1 million a year.

The offer was brusquely turned down by the Maldivian Government and Gan has now been leased to a Panama-based company called Scimitar for setting up an oil refinery. In any event, the Soviets would hardly find it politically profitable to instigate Male against New Delhi at this crucial stage in Indo-Soviet relations.

Implications: Nonetheless, the remarks are being interpreted as being embarrassing to India, particularly since they were made at an awkward moment. India is currently in the process of hammering out a maritime boundary agreement with Bangladesh after a frustrating series of aborted negotiations. Differences have been further exacerbated by that country's claim to the New Moore Islands. Bangladesh has so far refused to agree to the median line or equidistance principle according to which it would have to abandon claims to an area in the northern region of the Bay of Bengal where it has already given out concessions to foreign companies for oil exploration operations.

So far, agreements on maritime boundaries have been signed with Sri Lanka (1973), Indonesia (1977), Thailand (1978) and Maldives (1979). But no consensus has so far been reached with Bangladesh, Pakistan and Burma. Last fortnight, the Maldives Government once again reassured India that they were not laying claim to the Minicoys, and High Commissioner Kumar carried the same message when he flew in to New Delhi for talks with Foreign Minister Narasimha Rao and senior Foreign Ministry officials to brief them on the subject.

But the damage, albeit slight, seems to have been done — in the sense that Male's temporary muscle-flexing could provide Bangladesh, Burma and Pakistan with enough incentive to adopt a tougher stand on their own maritime boundary disputes with India.

—DILIP BOBB

Meemu to Laamu

One rarely sees or hears of *don mihun* around the central atolls, which is quite surprising for there is much to offer here in the way of scenery, history and culture. And getting to any of the islands in this region is no more difficult than getting to the other far-flung islands.

Meemu

Population	—	3,098
Inhabited Islands	—	9
Uninhabited Islands	—	26
Capital	—	Muli

As aforementioned, the Vattaru reef is one of the most popular and outstanding diving spots in the country, and, unbeknown to most visitors, just five kilometres south is an irregularly triangular chain of islands known traditionally as Mulaku, or commonly as Meemu.

Muli, the capital, is noted as the best place in the atoll when it comes to catching fish, and **Kolhufushi** and **Mulaku** are renowned for their agriculture, with yams growing profusely on both islands.

Faafu

Population	—	2,012
Inhabited Islands	—	5
Uninhabited Islands		21
Capital	—	Magoodhoo

South of Alifu atoll, beyond a 15km-wide, 230 fathom-deep channel, is a small oval-shaped chain of islands once known as the *uturu buri* of Nilandhoo, and now known as Faafu.

Daraboodhoo is by far the most outstanding island in these waters, foremost for its *kahambu*. During the *hulungu* monsoon you'll often see footprints along the beach and mounds of sand hidden beneath the bushes, the tell-tale sign that a turtle has laid her eggs. Sadly, these eggs invariably find their way to the *badige* (kitchen) where they end up as delicious sweet or savoury pikelets, and the *kahambu* finds its way to the tourist shop, stuffed or its shell in pieces. There are many locals here who claim *befalu* status, supposedly descendent from Muhammed Muhiddeen, a beloved 17th century Sultan.

Dhaalu

Population	— 3,003
Inhabited Islands	— 8
Uninhabited Islands	— 49
Capital	— Kudahuvadhoo

The *dekunu buri* of Nilandhoo is known administratively as Dhaalu, and it stretches some 35kms from north to south and 20kms across, just a little larger than its northern neighbour. And nationwide it is famed for its so-called "jewellers' islands".

In the northwest pocket of the atoll are the small villages of **Ribudhoo** and **Hulhudeli**, both housing many skilled craftsmen who employ age-old, subtle techniques and create gold and silver pendants, amulets, chains and bracelets. And the women on Ribudhoo are equally renowned for their skill at weaving thin strands of coir into thick *ras rornu*, the country's finest-quality "king rope".

Thaa

Population	— 6,224
Inhabited Islands	— 13
Uninhabited Islands	— 55
Capital	— Veymandhoo

Heading southwards across the Kudahuvadhoo *kandu* — or the Maa *kandu* as some travellers may call it — leads to a massive, almost

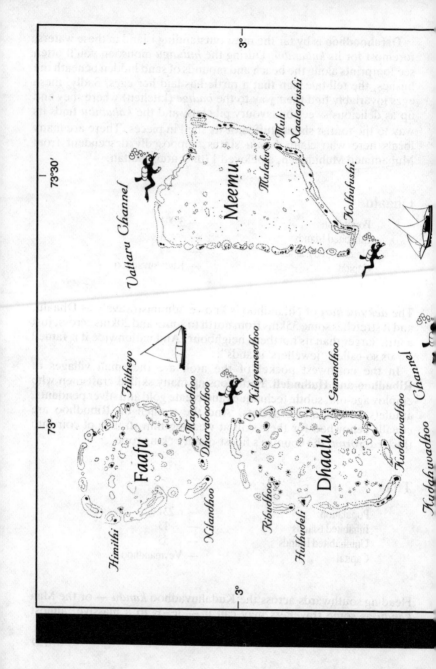

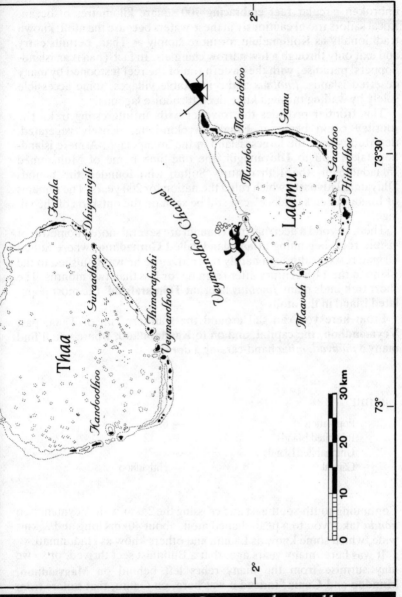

Central atolls

unbroken circular reef embracing 700 square kilometres of ocean. Local sailors travel cautiously in these waters because the atoll, known traditionally as Kolumadulu, or more simply as Thaa, permits entry and exit only through a few narrow channels. In fact Thaa is an island-hoppers' paradise, with the eastern rim of the reef festooned by many deserted islands, *finolhus* and remarkable villages, some accessible solely by wading through knee-deep turquoise lagoons.

This frontier provides the traveller with an interesting trek. The journey could begin at **Fahala**, a 6km-long, densely vegetated, deserted island, the largest island in the archipelago. A mere island-hop takes you to **Dhiyamigili**, the one-time home of Muhammed Imaaduddeen, the 18th century Sultan who founded the famous Dhiyamigili dynasty which ruled the nation for 200 years. The remains of Imaduddeen's "palace" can still be seen on the outskirts of the village.

Then, beyond a deep narrow channel are several more kilometres of visible reef, beginning at an island called **Guraadhoo**, where Sultan Usman rests — although hardly revered, since he was banished to the island in the 14th century after reigning for less than two months. The short trek ends many *finolhus* later, at **Thimarafushi**, the most populated island in the atoll.

From here you can sail around the southern rim of Thaa, past **Veymandhoo**, the capital, and on to **Kandoodhoo**, where you'll find many a *maavadi miha* hand-carving a *dorni*.

Laamu

Population	— 6,163
Inhabited Islands	— 12
Uninhabited Islands	— 71
Capital	— Hithadhoo

Continuing south-southeast and crossing the 25km-wide Veymandhoo *kandu* takes you to a pear-shaped atoll, about 40kms long and 25kms wide, which some know as Laamu and others know as Hadunmati.

It was here, many years ago, that a Buddhist sect thrived, or so we may surmise from the many relics left behind on **Maavaidhoo**, **Mundoo** and **Gamu**. Indeed it was here, on Gamu, that sailors from

the Indus Valley rested during their world tours nearly 4000 years ago
— or at least so says Thor Heyerdahl, the *Kon Tiki* explorer, who
visited the island in 1981, found slabs of coral with heiroglyphic script
and drawings of a Sun-God, and concluded that travellers knew of
these islands eons ago.

While these early-day travellers may indeed have passed by in their
reed ships, modern-day travellers will soon have the chance to fly there
in a Skyvan, for an airport is currently under construction at **Gaadhoo**,
on the southern tip of Laamu, and domestic flights are scheduled to
begin from Hulhule before the end of 1986.

The southern atolls

Not surprisingly the lifestyle is significantly different beyond the giant Huvadhoo *kandu*, the massive 85km-wide expanse of ocean — known popularly as the One and Half Degree Channel — that separates the central atolls from those further south. Here, there is little inter-dependence between the atolls, because they are each geographically isolated not only from the rest of the archipelago but also from each other, so it is fortunate that the climate is conducive to cultivating a variety of crops. Many of the islands, particularly around the Equatorial Channel, are more luxuriantly vegetated than their northern neighbours, with small plantations of bananas, yams, taro and manioc, as well as the ubiquitous coconut tree. And since every atoll is very much alone, isolated and largely self-sufficient it is perhaps not surprising to find obvious peculiarities in each atoll, the most outstanding being the spoken language. Pronunciation and vocabulary changes dramatically as one hops from atoll to atoll, so much so that there is a common agreement to speak Male *bas* (language) when a visitor from outside the atoll arrives on the island.

To visit these parts of the archipelago is to visit the Achilles' heel of the Maldives, because there has always been — and still is — an aloofness and inherent jealousy between islanders from the north and south. Until recently, in fact, the southerners traded directly with Sri Lanka, since it was equidistant to both Colombo and Male and they could always fetch a better price for their fish from the Sri Lankan merchants. At the same time they were endowed with some twenty years of western influence, with the British manning an air-base in Gan, the southernmost island, during the 1960s and '70s. A violent clash between north and south was therefore imminent when the government monopolised the export of fish and subsequently ordered the British to sack any southerners under their employ. Of course the attempted secession by the so-called "United Suvadive Islands" was doomed from the outset, but the feelings of their one-time President, Abdulla Afif Didi, still remain loud and clear in the minds of many people. His letter to the editor of the *London Times,* published when the secession was reaching its climax, is worth noting.

144

SITUATION IN THE MALDIVES

TO THE EDITOR OF THE TIMES

Sir, We have noted with interest statements in the Press and radio concerning the present political situation in the Maldives and in particular reports of the various utterances of the Male Government representatives in Ceylon and London. To present our side of the picture is the aim of this letter.

Some of our reasons for the secession from Male the old capital of the Maldives are as follows: The indifference of their administration to the elementary needs of the people of these islands food, clothing, medicine, education, social welfare, &c. For many years we have been reduced to serfs and bled by extortionate taxes and levies. At the commencement of this year further taxes were imposed and the people who had nothing left to give revolted.

Bear in mind we have not a single doctor for 18,000 undernourished people, nor any medical supplies whatsoever. We have no schools, no means of communication, no public utilities. All this is certainly the fault of Male. Epidemics of Asian flu, malaria, enteric, typhoid, diarrhoea, conjunctivitis, &c., sweep our islands periodically during the year, and in 1958 we had a serious outbreak of dysentery causing deaths. We appealed to Male for help. They refused and very piously told us to go on reading the Quran! The R.A.F. doctors came to our aid, supplied medicine and visited the sick day and night. Can you wonder that we hate Male ?

Our main export from these islands was dried Maldive fish which we sent to Male for sale in Ceylon. Payment was made to Male in Ceylon rupees but we were forced by Male to accept Maldivian rupees in return. One Maldivian rupee is worth only half a Ceylon rupee and we had then to buy what food we could afford from Male at Ceylon prices.

The presence of the British in Addu Atoll had absolutely nothing to do with the will of the people to break from Male. Attempts have been made before and as recently as 18 months ago men were imprisoned for trying to make an improvement. The R.A.F. at Gan Island had no knowledge of our intention to make an uprising on the first day of 1959 it was calculated action by the people to show Male that we are determined never again to submit to the despotic rule of a government of one family.

We wish to make it clear that we have set up a Government unanimously elected by the will of the people. We are a State of 18,000 people willing and able to support ourselves in spite of Male. We are now the United Suvadive Islands. Our immediate policy is betterment of our people, friendliness to all nations and in particular to the British who have sincerely helped and wisely guided the Maldives whenever we desired to do so in the past.

We are in favour of the staging post and radio station at Gan and Hitadu Islands respectively, which must bring economic development and prosperity to our islands. We earnestly appeal to your great and generous country and people for help and understanding. We have been inhabiting these islands from times immemorial, possessing thereby inalienable rights over them, the ownership thereof cannot certainly be claimed by the Male Government. We, therefore, appeal to the British Government to kindly grant us facilities to open negotiations at once with a view to conclude a Treaty of friendship and cooperation between her Majesty's Government and the United Suvadive Islands.

We hope the British Government and people will appreciate the justice of our cause and recognize the United Suvadive Islands at once. Yours truly,

ABDULLAH AFIF DIDI, President, United Suvadive Islands.
The Secretariat, Hitadu, United Suvadive Islands.

Other Correspondence : Page 9

Nowadays the ties between north and south, albeit strained, are somewhat strengthened. The remains of the RAF base (deserted since 1976) have now been converted into garment factories, restaurants and a so-called "holiday camp" for tourists, all under the watchful eye of the ADA, a special government department responsible for the economic welfare of the south, and answerable directly to the President. And there is a regular domestic flight between Hulhule and Gan, a flight which offers breathtaking sights as you skim low over the atolls for two hours. Book well in advance, however, because the flight is extremely popular with locals, even though the plane shakes and shudders and the *sifāng* serves only the obligatory refreshments of canned juice and dry biscuits. For more details refer to "Facts for the visitor".

Or alternatively you can hitch a ride on one of the many *vedis* which often cruise the 40 to 60 hour voyage between Male and the southernmost atolls. But it's only for the wildly adventurous who rough it with pleasure. It could be likened to riding an overcrowded Asian bus across the ocean waves, with passengers sardined between leaking oil drums, bursting suitcases, bicycles, chickens, vegetables, bawling children and an assortment of odds and ends. And of course there's the inevitable sea-sickness and the odd-man overboard. However, the fare is cheap, about Rf80 for the one-way trip with plenty of rice and curry for breakfast, lunch and dinner, and the boats are always easy to locate in the Male harbour — they lie deep in the water, weighed down with general cargo, and generally anchor near the Post Office. Consult the shipping agents in Male for more information, or contact the State Trading Organisation (STO) — behind the fruit and vegetable market — as they too operate a regular service, and charge only Rf50 one-way, meals included. Or better still ask Altaf Enterprises, operators of the holiday camp, to arrange a trip for you.

Gaafu Alifu

Population	— 4,978
Inhabited Islands	— 10
Uninhabited Islands	— 79
Capital	— Viligili

Following the eventual downfall of the southern secession the huge Huvadhoo (or Suvadive) atoll, the largest atoll in the world — 70kms long and 55kms wide — was split arbitrarily, for administrative purposes, in two — and called Gaafu Alifu and Gaafu Dhaalu.

The villages in the northern half, Gaafu Alifu, are scattered predominantly around the rim of the atoll, so it comes as no surprise to see the horizon, far beyond the reef, dotted with billowing sails as hundreds of *dornis* search for schools of deep-sea fish.

However there is a small village, **Dhevvadhoo**, at the centre of the the atoll, where fishing is not so prominent, as many of the 400-strong population have become famed for weaving cotton and coir.

Gaafu Dhaalu

Population	—	7,720
Inhabited Islands	—	10
Uninhabited Islands	—	150
Capital	—	Thinadhoo

The *dekunu buri* of Huvadhoo, nowadays called Gaafu Dhaalu, is both historically and culturally significant.

The present-day capital, **Thinadhoo**, was formerly the capital of the 249 islands which comprised Huvadhoo atoll, so it was inevitably in the limelight during the course of the southern rebellion. In fact, many locals still vividly recall the arrival, on February 4, 1962, of a fleet of armed government launches, and the ensuing battle when they met the Male *mihas'* guns with sticks, stones and verbal abuse — then the eventual declaration that the island was officially uninhabited and everyone sadly dispersing to nearby islands. And they also recall August 22, 1966, when they happily set sail back home, despite their rebellion being finally and fatally quashed. These times, however, are normally recalled in silence, for they still heed Ibrahim Nasir's advice that "the next door neighbour is your enemy", and it's best not to speak about politics and the past, far better indeed to speak of life's trivialities.

Nowadays when one thinks of Gaafu Dhaalu one thinks of *tandu kunaas,* the fine reed mats that are woven by the women from **Gadhoo**. There is no better souvenir than one of these two metre-long intricately woven mats, made from a reed called *ha* which grows profusely on a nearby uninhabited island, Fiyaori. Almost every house in Gadhoo, indeed many houses in neighbouring villages and atolls, has at least one of these mats, and if you offer Rf60 or more they may be

147

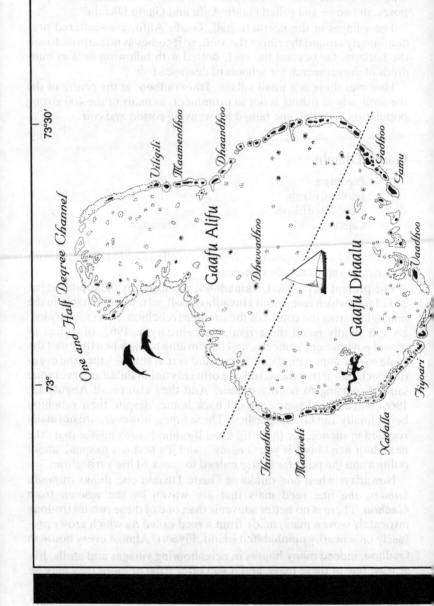

Southern atolls

tempted to sell — but remember, the mothers and grandmothers of these women were known to value their skills and refuse anything, even from the Sultan, but "a good price".

Vaadhoo, too, had its heyday, being the birthplace of Muhammed Ali, who reigned for eight years during the 17th century and did many special favours for his family and friends, not the least being the numerous mosques he built around Vaadhoo, some of them still standing today. And it was also the one-time home of Muhammed Jumaaluddin, a revered local sheikh who studied Islam overseas, before returning home to a regal welcome and, despite pleas that he become the nation's leading *gazi,* retiring to the life of a recluse in Vaadhoo. His tombstone is still periodically restored by the local *mudeem.*

Gnyaviyani

Population	—	4,204
Inhabited Islands	—	1
Uninhabited Islands	—	0
Capital	—	Fuamulak

Totally isolated in the midst of the Equatorial Channel, 40kms south of Gaafu Dhaalu and about 430kms from Male, is one of the archipelago's most notable atolls, Gnyaviyani — or **Fuamulak**, pronounced for-moo-luck, as it is more popularly known. It is a single island, 6kms long, surrounded by a steep, coarse coral shingle beach and densely vegetated, with a wide variety of tropical vegetables and fruits, many of them, such as pineapples and oranges, growing nowhere else in the country. It is widely reputed that despite their isolation the 4,000-plus population has a much greater lifespan than any of their neighbours, a fact largely attributed to the healthy island-diet and climate. Because of its isolation Fuamulak has for many years been an ideal destination for political prisoners.

During his visit to Fuamulak in 1922, H.C.P. Bell discovered a stone head of Buddha, a crystal casket and a few oval beads, and still today the visitor can find some ancient monuments.

To orientate oneself to the island it's worth noting that there are several suburbs, namely: Dhadi Magu, Dhiguvaadu, Hoadadhu, Miski Magu, Malegamu, Dhoodigamu and Funaadu.

Seenu

Population	— 29,555
Inhabited Islands	— 6
Uninhabited Islands	— 27
Capital	— Hithadhoo

About three hours' cruising from Fuamulak — or nearly 600kms from Male — is the southernmost atoll in the Maldives, Seenu. For many years, particularly during the rebellious 1960s, it was regarded as the economic and political hub of the southernmost atolls and still today the inhabitants refer to themselves proudly as *Addu mihun* (after the traditional name of their atoll), rather than *Divehin*. It therefore comes as no surprise that the government, today, concentrates much of its attention here, in efforts to appease the southerners for the life-style denied them after the British vacated their air-base on **Gan** in 1976.

Nowadays a scheduled domestic flight links Seenu with Male and the former RAF officers' barracks on Gan have been converted into a 20-room holiday camp with all the resort-type facilities, including a professionally-operated diving school. Rates are around $30/35 for singles/doubles. Reservations should be made through Altaf Enterprises, 8 Ahmedi Bazaar, Male (tel: 3378, tlx: 66047 Altaf). Although the island cannot boast any spectacular natural beauty or long stretches of sandy shoreline and shallows, its attractions are nonetheless unique and include many legacies left behind by the British — a swimming pool and tennis court, an overgrown 18-hole golf course and, perhaps most significantly, the English language, which is spoken, sometimes fluently, throughout the atoll. And of course there's a floating population of several hundred locals who come and go every day, to work at the garment factories near the camp.

Moreover, getting around the atoll is cheap and simple, since many of the villages are accessible from Gan by road — the 15km-long road that extends via causeways and villages to the northwestern tip of the atoll.

Leaving Gan by foot — or on the 4pm factory bus — takes you across a causeway (built by the British in 1970) to **Feydhoo**, a densely populated village of 2,300 people. If you care to rest a while go direct to Venus Vilaa, a small tea shop on the main *magu,* where the owner will quickly offer you a *kalu sā* and short-eats, and a short history on life in Seenu.

Continuing beyond Feydhoo, across another small, narrow causeway, leads to a similar style village called **Maradhoo**. The *bodu miha* of the village owns a fleet of *dornis,* leases Viligili, a nearby uninhabited island , and has a two-storey house on the main *magu,* which he reserves for visiting VIPs.

Further on, past the village and across another causeway, begins several kilometres of wide open grassland and magnificent coastline, once used by the British as the site of their Earth Station, and now the best place in Seenu to get away from it all, to laze and bask in the sun and swim and snorkel around the lagoon.

Pedalling northward brings you finally to **Hithadhoo**, the capital, and a densely populated island of 6000 people. It was here that Abdullah Afif Didi masterminded the attempted secession and still today the visitor is immediately aware of the island's influential, affluent undertones. Large *magus* and charming colonial-style coral houses beautify the village, many families enjoy the luxury of electricity, the *bodu mihun* own fleets of *dornis* and *vedis,* and all forms of traditional pastimes — fishing, weaving, toddy-tapping, carpentry and gold and silver jewellery-making — are undertaken. And there are many isolated sandy coves where one can escape and be alone.

A tour of Seenu is not complete, however, without a visit to **Hulhumeedhoo**, on the eastern fringe of the atoll. The lifestyle in the village is always a source of entertainment with much bickering and jealousy continually on show. In fact, since July 1, 1975 the population has officially been separated into two villages,with the southern half, Hulhudhoo, claiming to be far more active and industrious than their neighbours in Meedhoo, who in turn boast a pious outlook on life and meticulously preserve an ancient tombstone on the outskirts of their village, which they say (though no one believes them) belongs to the original founding-father of Islam in the Maldives. While you're here you can wade through the ankle-deep lagoon to **Herethere**, a long-deserted ilsand which is ideal for camping overnight.

So in a nutshell, and despite the fact that there are better beaches, lagoons and underwater scenery in the Maldives, Seenu is an outstandingly different destination, one perfectly suited to the traveller who enjoys travel for travel's sake. Expect the unexpected and a visit to Seenu will be a pleasurable experience.

Superpowers at Bay
India Today, September 1, 1981

In March 1976, after a long running feud with the Maldivian people who wanted them out of their idyllic islands, the British had a final pink gin at their exclusive club, packed their bags and quit Gan, the southernmost of 2,000 exotic Maldive islands. No sooner had they left their World War II vintage staging post, than this strategic island of swaying coconut trees and incredibly blue lagoons 1,440 km southwest of Trivandrum was up for grabs. It had plenty going for it.

Almost on the equator, Gan dominated the strategic sea lanes of the troubled Indian Ocean just as effectively as Diego Garcia, 800km away. What is more, there was already a large airstrip, port facilities, a hospital, a botanical garden, not forgetting the club and the golf course.

Rattled by the prospective American buildup on Diego Garcia, the most serious offer predictably came from the Russians. "They offered the Maldivian Government one million dollars annually for repair and recreation facilities for their Indian Ocean fishing fleet" recalled Abbas Ibrahim, the Maldivian president's executive secretary. "But after much discussion, the Maldivian Cabinet finally said no. We wanted a non-aligned foreign policy and a peaceful Indian Ocean".

Nevertheless, as both superpowers tried to muscle in, the question mark over Gan's future remained — till last month. In an Id speech in Addu Atoll of which lovely Gan is a part, the slightly-built and dapper President Maumoon Abdul Gayoom said, "We shall not lease Gan for any military purposes. We are in the non-aligned movement, and we believe no non-aligned country can have any military bases within its territory". Revealing that two recent foreign offers to lease Gan were being considered, the one time university professor added that the Government would negotiate with any party ready to co-operate with it in developing Gan only as an economic and commercial base.

Economic Proposals: Leasing Gan for economic purposes is not a new idea. It acquired considerable urgency ever since the British left — with all the island's jobs and Abdulla Afeef Didi, a rebel Addu leader they had encouraged to secede. Thousands were thrown out of work, and descended *en masse* on the capital Male, creating tension and social problems in a country of 150,000 people. In 1977, the Government advertised in Hong Kong newspapers. Various companies came up with proposals, but weren't found to be suitable. Repeating the advertisements two years later in London's prestigious *Financial Times* proved equally infructuous.

Early this year the Government thought of doing something on its own, and formed the Addu Development Authority. The Maldives State Trading Organisation, collaborating with Hong Kong and Singapore entrepreneurs, has already set up two garment factories. Many more are likely to come. "The factories, producing clothes exclusively for the US, are merely a means to get around the exhausted US garment quotas set for Hong Kong and Singapore", a top official confided. "They are really doing a finishing job, like tacking on shirt sleeves. But the legend reads 'Made in Maldives'." Gan is also being developed for tourism, and regular commercial flights from Male are on the cards. At present they're only available twice a week.

Meanwhile, though officially relations between the Indian and Maldivian Governments are stated to be excellent (Indian Airlines has run Maldive International Airlines for several years now), there is considerable suspicion of India's intentions to dominate the region. "This fear has been spread in part by subversive literature distributed by the Pakistan Embassy working overtime", Ibram conceded, "but there is the example of Sikkim and India's role in Pakistan's break-up." Though addicted to Indian films and popular music, he hinted that the wholly Muslim island strongly identifies with Pakistan and reacts similarly though less vocally to Indian communal riots.

Resentment: Adding to the apprehension and resentment are Indian shopkeepers, who dominate Male's main market and outhustle their slack Maldivian counterparts. Till 1959 trade and indeed the Government was dominated by Indian Bohras who left when foreigners were banned from doing business. The 1976 lifting of the ban saw the Bohras replaced in trade by Sindhis. Indian tourists, wittingly or not, wind up in their shops — to receive among other things excellent advice on what will pass Indian customs — creating resentment.

Duty-free Male is a key supply point for smuggling into India and 'tourists' from India have doubled since last year. However, most of these are unlikely candidates for sun-bathing, skin-diving or indeed the underwater shark circus at Bandos Island. Lugging heavy suitcases, these young carriers immediately head for the bazaar and begin open discussions on the price fluctuation in electronic goods, fabric and perfumes.

Maldivian government officials disclose that there is a lot of smuggling into India and Sri Lanka by boat as well. Gayoom, when asked about the ubiquitous South African products in the market, blandly replied, "The Government does not import them, private traders do." Given that live and let live approach, the pavement hawkers at Bombay's Flora Fountain have little to worry about.

— ARUN CHACKO

The Maldivian language

During your travels in the Maldives, even if they only take you along the well-worn tourist trails, a knowledge of *Divehi*, the local language, could prove invaluable. Here are some words and phrases to help you along the way.

Pronunciation

a	as in	c**u**t
e	as in	r**e**d
i	as in	f**i**t
o	as in	h**o**t
u	as in	p**u**t
aa	as in	f**a**ther
ai	as in	**eye**
ā	as in	b**a**t
ee	as in	tr**ee**

Greetings and civilities

hello	salaam alekum
how are you?	haalu kihine?
not bad	nubā nu
very well	vara gada
good	rangalu
I'm going	Aharen dani
see you later	goslani
thank you	sukuria

Small talk

what's the matter?	kihine vi?
it doesn't matter	kame nu
what did you say?	kike?

what's happening?	kihine vani?
where are you going?	kong taka dani?
wait there	etang hure
come here	mitang ade
where; why	korba; kivi
who; what	kaaku; korche
understand	enge
don't know	nenge
yes; no	aa; nu

Personal talk

who is that?	e kaaku?
those people	e mihun
who is this?	mi kaaku?
I; me; you	Aharen; ma; kale
he; she	ena; mina
man; woman	firihen; anhen
father; mother	bapa; mama
uncle; aunt	bodu bebe; bodu data
brother; sister	bebe; data
son; daughter	darifalu
friend	rātehi
close friend	rahumatehi

Ge is also a useful word to know, it turns a noun into a pronoun eg. *ma* (me) becomes *mage* (my).

Time

what time is it?	gadi kihaiaru?
Sunday	Aadita
Monday	Horma
Tuesday	Angaara
Wednesday	Buda
Thursday	Brassfati
Friday	Hukuru
Saturday	Honihiru
yesterday	iye
today	miadu
tonight	mire

157

tomorrow	maadama
dawn	fatihu
sunrise	iru arani
morning	hendunu
midday	menduru
afternoon	haviru
sunset	iru osani
evening	regandu
two o'clock	de jahairu
quarter past three	tin gadi fanara
half past nine	nua gadi bā
before	kuring
now	miharu
after	fahung
in a little while	tankuli fahung
day	duvas
week	hafta
month	mas duvas
year	aharu

Numbers

1	eke	6	haie
2	de	7	hate
3	tine	8	ashe
4	hatare	9	nue
5	fahe	10	diha
11	egaara	16	sorla
12	baara	17	satara
13	tera	18	ashara
14	saada	19	onavihi
15	fanara	20	vihi
30	tiris	90	nua-diha
40	saalis	100	sateka
50	fansaas	200	de-sateka
60	fasdolaas	300	tin sateka
70	hai-diha	400	hatare-sateka
80	a-diha	500	fas-sateka

1000	en-haas	100,000	elaka
10,000	diha-haas	zero	sume

At the market

how much is this?	mi kihavaraka?
what is that?	e korche?
expensive	agu bodu
cheap	agu heo
fruit	meva
vegetables	tarukari
fish	mas
banana	donkeo
mango	ambu
papaya	falor
breadfruit	bambukeo
pumpkin	barabor
cabbage	korpi
chilli	mirus
lentils	mugu
rice (raw)	handu
coconut (old)	kaashi
onions	fia
garlic	lonumedu

Around the Male market and on the far-flung islands it is common to come across the Maldivian measurements for grains and liquids. The *laahi* is the most commonly used, and usually comes in the form of a 250g condensed milk container or an equivalent-size coconut shell. Four *laahi* of rice is a *naali,* and four of honey is an *adubaa.* Measuring lengths of material involves terms like *mu* and *rian.*

Two very common words in day-day-to-day conversation are *ta* and *dor.* Both turn a statement into a question. *Ebahuri ta* means "do you have?", and *ebahuri dor* is "you have, don't you?"

Enge is another word you will hear quite often. It is used at the end of a sentence, seemingly to make sure the other person is listening. For example, *Aharen dani, enge* — "I'm going, OK?".

And remember, too, the market is a place for bargaining, so confidently sprout a few exclamations if you think the price is too high — *ekamakva* is a popular expression. It's similar to "good grief!".

In the restaurant

what is there to eat?	kaa-etche korba?
rice (cooked)	bai
unleavened bread	roshi
curry	riha
tea (black)	kalu sā
(white)	kiru sā
(no sugar)	hakuru naalang
short-eats	sā-etche
knife	vali
spoon	samsaa
fork	or
that's enough	denheo
a little bit more	adi kuda eti kolu
not too chilli hot	kuli madu
tasty	raha miru
bad taste	raha nubā
dahl curry	mugu riha
vegetable curry	tarukari riha
cold drink	fini bor eche
drinking water	bor feng
much too sweet	maa foni gada
I'm hungry	Aharen bandufā
I'm thirsty	Aharen feng borvāgatung
I'm full	Aharen bandu budu vejje
sit here!	mitang ishinde!
a good restaurant	rangalu horta

Travelling around

when do you leave?	furani kong iru kung?
how long does it take?	devene kita duvas?
will you take me?	gengos denangta?
good wind	vā rangalu
a bad current	oia nubā
I'm sea-sick	Aharen kandu bali
what's that island?	e ra korche?
how much is the fare?	fi kihavaraka?

160

is it time to go?	furang vejje ta?
bon voyage	hing heo kurati
hoist the sail!	ria naga!

Place names

Newcomers are often confused by the long tongue-twisting island names, but when considered in parts they are not quite so indecipherable.

For example, *Meerufenfushi,* meeru-fen-fushi, is sweet-water-island; *Makunufushi,* makunu-fushi, is bed bug-island; and *Anhenfushi,* anhen-fushi, is woman's-island. Some islands have meaning according to a foreign language, such as Hindi or Sinhala. *Maafilaafushi* is derived from the Maappilas, a Moslem caste from India, and *Lankanfushi* is, of course, borrowed from Sri Lanka.

As for the atoll names, they too are tongue-twisters. But in the 1940s, for ease of administration, traditional atoll names were assigned letters of the alphabet, hence today it is quite common to hear both the traditional and administrative nuances when referring to the atolls. Therefore it is worth noting both, from north to south:

traditional name	administrative name
North Tiladunmati	Haa Alifu
South Tiladunmati	Haa Dhaalu
North Miladunmadulu	Shaviyani
South Miladunmadulu	Noonu
North Maalosmadulu	Raa
South Maalosmadulu	Baa
Faadippolu	Laviyani
Male	Kaafu
Ari	Alifu
Felidhoo	Vaavu
Mulaka	Meemu
North Nilandhoo	Faafu
South Nilandhoo	Dhaalu
Kolumadulu	Thaa
Hadunmati	Laamu
North Huvadhoo	Gaafu Alifu
South Huvadhoo	Gaafu Dhaalu
Fuamulak	Gnyaviyani
Addu	Seenu

161

Glossary

Local terms have been used quite frequently in this book and many more will be heard, however and wherever you travel in the Maldives.

ADA Addu Development Authority.

aduba a measurement of fluid, equivalent to four *laahi*.

aigaadia a pushcart used for transporting luggage and cargo in Male.

assara a side-dish to rice and curry, more often than not a mixture of onion, chilli and lime juice.

atiri mati the locals often ask *kong taka dani?* — where are you going? — and as I was usually on my way to the beach, I would reply *atiri mati* which never failed to invite squeals of laughter. Later I was to learn that this expression meant you were off to perform a few natural duties on the beach, and not, as I thought, to go to the beach with the intention of swimming.

atolu verin the atoll chief, responsible for the economic and political welfare of his administrative atoll.

badige usually a small, thatch-roofed coral room with no windows, separate from the living quarters and containing no more than a bare limestone floor with two or three dug-outs for stoves, a stack of firewood, some pots, pans and home-carved wooden cooking utensils. And fillets of boiled fish smoking over a burnt-out fire. It's the kitchen, and despite the heat and fumes, many women, indeed whole families, simply squat on the floor to eat their meals.

bandia jehang the popular, traditional dance performed by young girls who writhe as they tap out a rhythm on metal water pots called *bandia.*

bas language.

bateli the high-bowed *dornis,* around twenty metres long, many with two masts and a deckhouse, some propelled by inboard engines, others by lateen cloth sails, and most of them used for long-distance travelling.

bati a battery-operated lamp available for less than Rf10 from most island stores and a must if you're riding a bicycle after dark. They are also very handy to have in your luggage for those dark moonless nights in the far-flung villages where there is no electricity.

befalu the so-called "noble class", the close friends and relatives of the former Sultans.

bidi a popular "cigarette" made from newspaper and a dark brown imported tobacco leaf. Probably has a lot to do with the average life-span being only 50.5 years!

bile a strong-tasting green leaf, eaten after and between meals with arecanut and spices.

bimbi a locally-grown black millet, regarded as a "poor man's food" despite its nutritional value. It is extremely tasty.

bodu beru a drum made from hollowed coconut wood and the hide of a stingray.

borki a kerosene pressure lamp or electric light bulb.

daani a small aluminium can attached to a long stick, used to take water from the well and for showering.

dandi jehang similar to the *bandia jehang,* except that it is performed by men beating time with sticks.

darifalu offspring.

daturu voyage.

dekunu buri the southern part.

dia hakuru smooth, golden coconut honey made by cooking and stirring *raa* for several hours.

Divehi the spoken language.

Divehin means "islander", and is the appellation used for all Maldivians.

Divehi Rajje the "Island Kingdom", the local term for the Maldives.

don miha literaly means "white man" and generally applies to all tourists (although if you have black skin, you are more likely to be called *kalu be* — "black brother"). Some tourists may be affectionately called *don be* and others may be respectfully referred to as *don Maniku* (for men) or *don Kamana* (for women). Pale skin is the envy of all locals, but if you happen to have blonde hair you'll be considered *muskuli* (old).

dufani chewing *bile* and *for*.

faatiha a memorial service for a deceased friend or family member.

fandita a sort of religious science.

fang cadjan, made by threading dried palm leaves together with rope.

faru a shallow lagoon.

fatali hakuru a sweet toffee-creamed honey made by cooking and stirring for hours the sweet *raa,* with liberal additions of sugar.

fihara the island store, often no more than a small room in someone's house, usually lined with shelves of condensed milk, cordial, toothpaste, sweets and shampoo (if you're lucky), and sacks of rice flour and sugar. Beyond Male, the stores put a 10% mark-up on their prices.

finolhu a sandbank with little or no vegetation.

for arecanut, usually eaten with *bile*.

fulibati a small glass jar, a strip of recycled aluminium, and a piece of thread suspended in kerosene, provides a flickering light which burns all night in most homes. A local invention.

garudia fish broth, best eaten with rice, a piece of boiled fish, *assara* and a dash of *rihaakuru*.

gazi the locally-trained Islamic judge who presides over common matters like marriage, divorce and petty crime. A man of high repute in the village community.

gifili the local-style bathroom. A high (by Maldivian standards) coral or thatched fence surrounding a small garden of plants, trees and shrubs and a deep-water well.

Giraavaru the aborigines, said to be descended from the Indian Tamils but also believed (by some academics) to be from the same tribe as the Australian aborigines.

golhi usually a narrow lane running off a wide *magu*.

goti the 15 x 30 metre family property, granted by the government to all families.

hadith the sayings of Prophet Muhammed, regarded as a supplement to the scriptures, the Quran.

haji the title acquired by anyone who accomplishes the ultimate Islamic goal: the *hijra*.

hakeem the local medicine man.

hejira Muhammed's flight from Mecca to Medina in 622AD. The Muhammedan era and the Islamic calendar are reckoned from this time.

higun much like a *golhi,* but a little longer and wider.

hijra the pilgrimage to Mecca, made by only a few affluent citizens, or those who are assisted by the government. It is the Arab word meaning "departure from one's country".

hiki mas rock-hard fillets of tuna, popularly known as "Maldive fish". Thin slices of *hiki mas* eaten with chunks of *kaashi* is a popular snack.

hulungu the southwest monsoon.

iloshi fati hundreds of coconut leaves are stripped to their thin flexible spine, then tied together to form a broom. It is particularly effective on sand floors and the women can be seen at any time of day, backs bent, sweeping the roads, their yards, and the mosques, until once again the island is neat and tidy.

iruva the northeast monsoon.

Islam the youngest, one of the largest, and the fastest growing religion in the world.

jinni the demonic spirits that seek to do harm to mankind, or lead man astray.

jorli a hammock-like chair found outside most homes, or suspended from trees. A great place to relax and dream.

kaashi an old coconut, used in cooking.

kaashi kiru coconut milk, made by soaking grated coconut in water and squeezing out the pulp, and used as the base in curries.

kahambu the female turtle, often seen floating around the coral reefs and sometimes lumbering along the island shores.

karu hakuru a thick, creamy-white honey made by cooking *dia hakuru* with added sugar. There are many grades, the quality depending on the strength of the cook in charge of stirring.

kanamadu a nutritious nut which grows wild on many islands.

kandiki the black skirt worn under a *libaas*.

kandu a channel of deep blue sea.

kandu mas skipjack, easily identified by its long thin stripes.

kaneli yellowfin tuna, usually the largest of the tuna species.

kateeb the island chief, elected every two years.

keolu the captain of a fishing crew.

kuda kateeb the deputy island chief.

kudi-bai a locally-grown brown millet which the Maldivians rarely eat. It's a must for cous cous connoisseurs.

kurumba a young coconut, ideal for drinking.

laahi a standard measure of grain or liquids, equivalent to roughly 250 grams of rice or about 9 fluid ounces of honey.

lati mackerel tuna, has the darkest flesh of all the tuna species and is easily identified by three spots near the pectoral fin.

libaas the long-sleeved, brightly coloured dress worn by the women over a *kandiki*. It is worn tight across the arms and chest and loose around the stomach and legs, so whether the woman is active, inactive or pregnant makes little difference.

lonu mas fillets of fish coated with salt and left to dry in the sun. It's found everywhere and although it's not eaten at all by the locals it is exported in large quantities, to neighbouring countries.

maavadi miha a carpenter.

maavaharu ambergris, from the gut of the sperm whale. An extremely valuable substance used in the manufacture of expensive perfumes and cosmetics, and sometimes found along the island shores.

madiri dundandi mosquito coils, available from most island stores and a must in every traveller's luggage.

magu a wide unpaved coral street.

makthab traditional, privately-owned Quranic schools which teach young island children to read and write Divehi and Arabic and do simple arithmetic.

Male miha the term affectionately or otherwise used when referring to a resident of Male.

mas fish .

miski usually no more than a large coral building with a corrugated iron roof, but in effect a mosque.

maalud a Moslem lore recital.

MSL Maldive Shipping Limited, the national shipping line. Although head office is in Male, the operations are entirely managed from Singapore, by Umar Maniku, one of the most affluent and influential Maldivian citizens. MSL operates more than forty tankers and trawlers which ply regularly between Europe and the Far East.

mu about 13½ inches, a standard linear measurement most often used when buying cloth materials.

mudeem the meuzzin or island prayer-caller.

mundu a sarong, the traditional male attire.

nakai an interval of 13 or 14 days when the weather is fairly consistent.

oi the ocean current, runs nationwide at an average speed of 25 metres per minute.

Quran the revelations of Prophet Muhammed, as translated from the bones, stones, leaves and parchment on which they were originally written. It is the ultimate authority for Moslems on how God, or Allah, expects man to live.

raa the deliciously sweet toddy, tapped from the coconut trees.

raaveri a toddy-tapper.

ragondi bluefin tuna, usually found wherever there's a flock of birds hovering close to the ocean surface.

raivaru a sort of poetic chant.

raveri anyone who leases an uninhabited island.

rian about 27 inches, or approximately the length of an adult's arm from fingertip to shoulder blade. It's a standard Maldivian measure, used when building boats.

rihaakuru dark brown concentrated fish-paste made by the continual boiling down of large amounts of garudia, fish and salt.

rornu coir rope, made from the stringy insides of coconut husks after they've been buried in sand for several days.

roshi unleavened bread.

sā tea, the national beverage.

saanti a soft latticed mat woven from thin strips of dried screwpine reed, usually about 2 metres long.

sā-eche the sweet and savoury short-eats which are served with tea.

salavat a popular religious ritual often practised as a deterrent to *jinnis*.

sariatu the Islamic legal code, the only system of justice in the Maldives.

sifāng policemen, easily identified by their uniform: long trousers and white shirts with narrow black trimming.

STO State Trading Organisation.

sutuli the best type of thread for a *fulibati*.

Taana the local script.

Tarikh a history of the Maldivian Sultans, originated by Hasan Tajaldin, continued by his nephew, completed by his grandson and later destroyed when the Sultan's palace was burned down in 1752. A copy has since been prepared but it is as yet unavailable to the public, hence academics rely on a translated copy prepared by H.C.P. Bell.

undorli a wooden, swinging bed found under huge breadfruit trees in many *gotis*.

us fas gandu a mound of coral debris, invariably the burial ground of some ancient Buddhist relics and only found on a handful of islands.

uturu buri the northern part.

vali a knife, made in all shapes and sizes from a small *mas vali* used for cutting fish to a large *kata vali* used for collecting firewood. Children learn to handle knives at a very early age.

yacht-dorni a locally-built coconut wood boat with a large wooden cabin, usually with facilities for sleeping and cooking.

Dictionary

For that typical occurrence, when you need only a word to get across a thought, the following word-list may come in handy.

above	matiga	baby	la kudja
ache, to	riheni	backbone	mabada
acid	aavi	bacon	uru mas
across	huras	bad	nubā
active	muraali	bag	dabas, kotalu
advice	nasehai	bail, to	hikani
advertisement	istihaaru	bait	eng
aeroplane	matindaa bortu	bake, to	fihani
after	fahung	balance	hama hama
afternoon	menduru	balloon	fupa hang
again	alung	banana — yellow	donkeo
age	umuru	— cooking	maluskeo
airgun	vā-badi	barbeque, to	fihani
alcohol	bangu raa	barber	bor koshaa miha
all	muling	basket	vashi gandu
also	ves	bastard	nahalaalu
anchor	nagili	bathe, to	feng vurani
ancient	evela	beach	atiri
angel	malaaikatu	beacon	dile bati
angry	ruli	bean	toli
animal	janavaaru	beard	tumbuli
ankle	kuda hulu	beautiful	reeti
anniversary	munaasiba	bed	endu
annoy, to	undagu kurani	bed-bug	tai makunu
answer	javaab	beef	geri mas
ant	hini	beer	biaru
anyone	kome mihaku	before	kuriga, kuring
anything	kome eche	beg, to	salaam jehani
apply, to	laani	begin, to	fashani
arm	ai	believe, to	gabul kurani
ascend, to	macha arani	bellows	girumbaa
arsenic	korkadi	belongings	taketi
ash	ali	below	tiriga
ash-tray	ali-kendi	beside	kariga
ask, to	ahang	best	evana
astrology	nakai terikang	betel-leaf	bile
attire	hedung	-nut	for

171

between	demedu	cage	koshi
bicycle	basikalu	cake	keku
big	bodu	calm	madu
bird	duni	call, to	govani
birthday	ufang duvas	camphor	kaafuru
bite, to	daing alani	can	dalu
bitter	hiti	candle	ubati
black	kalu	cannot	nuvaane
blade	tila	captain	nevi kalege
blanket	rajaa	cardamon	kaafurutoli
blind	kanu	cargo	aagu
blood	le	castigate, to	bavani
blow, to	fumani	cat	bulaa
blue	nu kula	ceiling	fangi filaa
blue-bottle	firuvaanu muda	certain	yaging, gāmu
blunt	koshi	chair	gondi
body	gā	change, to (money)	maaru kurani
boil, to	kakani	cheap	agu heo
bone	kashi gandu	cheat	makaru
book	foi	cheek	kor
bottle	fuli	chef	bifaanu
bow (of ship)	kuri kolu	chess	raazuva
bowels	kuda gohoru	chest	urumati
box	foshi	chew, to	hafani
bracelet	ula	chicken	kukulu
brain	sikondi	child	kuja
bread	paan	chilli	mirus
breadfruit	bambukeo	– dry	hiki mirus
breakfast	handunu sā	– raw	ror mirus
breast	kiru	chin	daidoli
breathe, to	nevaalani	chisel	vadang kashi
bright	ali gada	cholera	hodu rorga
bring, to	genani	chop, to	koshani
broad	fula	cigar	suta
broom	iloshi fati	cinnamon	fonitoshi
brush	burus	circumcise, to	hitaanu kurani
build, to	alani, raanani	clean	saaf
burn, to	andani	clean, to	saafu kurani
bury, to	valulani	closed	lapaafa
but	ekamaku	close, to	lapani
butter	bataru	clothes	hedung
butterfly	korka	cloves	karamfu
button	gor	cock	haa

coconut – young	kurumba
– old	kaashi
– scrapings	kaashi huni
– tree	ru
– shell	naashi
coffee	kofi
coffin	sandor
cold	fini
colour	kula
comb	funaa
come, to	anani
comfort	araamu
common	aadāge
compass	samuga
condensed milk	geri kiru
constipation	bodu kamu nudevung
container	alaa eche
contract	ebasvung
cook, to	kakani
copper	ratulor
copy, to	nakalu kurani
coral	akiri
– black	enderi
corpse	gaburu
cotton wool	kafa
cough, to	kesani
count, to	gunani
country	rajje
cow	geri
cowrie	kuda boli
crab – land	baraveli
– sea	kakuni
crazy	moia
create, to	hadani
crime	ku
crooked	gudu
crow	kalu
cruel	ihaaneti
cry, to	rornani
cucumber	bodu kekuri
cunning	makaru
cup	jordu
cupboard	alimaari

curry	riha
– paste	havaadu
custard apple	ata
cut, to	kandani
damaged	halaakvi
dance, to	nashani
danger	nuraka
dark	andiri
dates	kaduru
dawn	fatihu
dead	maruveje
debt	darani
deep	fung
demonstration	muzaahiraa
dentist	daijaha miha
desire, to	umid kurani
devil	iblis
dew	sabnam
diarrhoea	bera hingun
die, to	maruvani
different	tafaatu
difficult	undagu
dig, to	konani
dirty	hadi
disgraceful	huturu
dish	tashi
distance	duruming
dive, to	feenani
divide, to	bābā kurani
divorce	varive
do, to	kurani
dog	kuta
dolphin	kormas
donkey	himaaru
door	bodu doru
doubt	saku
down	tiri
dragon-fly	lorfindu
draw, to	kurahani
dream	huvafeng

173

drill	buruma	fall, to	vetani
drink, to	boni	family	owlaadu
drum	beru	famous	masuru
dry	hiki	fan	fanka
duck	asduni	fantastic	faka
dumb	mamanu	far	duru, duruga
		fare	fi
		fast	bara
ear	kanfai	fasten, to	asani
early	avas	fat	fala
earth	bing	fate	iraada
east	irumati	fear	biru
eat, to	kani	feather	fai
eel	veng	feel, to (think)	hivani
egg	bis	feet	fātila
eggplant	bashi	fever	hung
elbow	ulam bashi	few	madu
empty	husvi	field	dandu
end	kolu	fight, to	hifani
enemy	hasada veria	find, to	hordani
enough	heo	finger	ingili
enter, to	vanani	finished	nimuni
envelope	siti ura	fire	alifang
equal	evaru	firewood	daru
evening	regandu	first	evana
everything	hurihaa eche	fish	mas
exact	baraabaru	fish, to	mas baanani
example	misaalu	fishing line	vadunanu
exchange, to	badalu kurani	flag	dida
exit	nukuna tang	flat	fataa
expense	haradu	flip-flops	fāvang
expensive	agu bodu	floor	bingmati
extinct	neti vediung	flour	godang
extinguish, to	nivani	flour-sifter	fufurene
eye	lor	flower	maa
eyebrow	buma	fly	mehi
eyelash	esfia	forehead	ni
eyelid	lolubondi	foreigner	bera miha
		forget, to	handaang netuni
		frog	bor
		front	kuri
face	munumati	fry, to	telani
fair (skin)	don	full	furifa, furijje

game	kulivaru	have, to	huri
garbage	kuni	head	bor
garden	bagicha	headbug	ukunu
garlic	lonumedu	healthy	sihaatu
gentle	madu maitiri	heart	hi
get away	dura de	heat, to	hunu kurani
get out	nukume	heaven	suvaruge
get up	teduve	heavy	baru
ghee	gitio	heel	funaabu
ghekko	hornu	hell	narukai
gift	hadia	herbs	faipilaaveli
ginger	inguru	heron	maakana
give, to	denani	hide, to	feelani
glass	biluri	high	us
glove	ura	hold, to	hifaatani, hifani
glue	teras	holiday	bandu duvas
go, to	dani	home	ge
goat	bakari	honour	aburu
gold	rang	hook (fish)	buli
grin	fuke	horizon	udares
grass	vina	horse	as
green	fehi kula	hot – temperature	hunu
grey	ali kula	– chilli	kuli
grill, to	fihani	house	ge
grind, to	fundani	how	kihine
grow, to	hadani	– much	kihavaraka
government	sarukaaru	– many	kita
guava	feru	hit, to	jahani
guilty	baazaaruvi	hungry	bandufā
gums	hiru	hurry	avas
gun	badi	hurt	tadu

hair	istashi	ice	gandu feng
half	bā	idiot	kos miha
hammer	maruteo	ill	bali
hang, to	eluvani	illegal	manaa
hand	aitila	if	nama
handkerchief	kuda rumaa	image	sura
handsome	chaalu	incense	dungdoli
happy	ufaa	infection	nubāvung
hard	haru	ink	deli
hat	taakia	inheritance	vaaruta

innocent	teduveri	learn, to	das kurani
inside	etere	leave, to	furani
insult	badanaamu	leg	fã
intelligent	visnung gada	legitimate	haalaalu
into	eterea	leisure	araam
invisible	nufenang	lentils	mugu
invitation	dowvat	letter	siti
iron	daagandu	lid	mati
island	ra	lies	dogu
		lie down, to	orshornani
		life	hiyaat
jar	fuli	light	ali
jasmine	huvandu maa	lightweight	lui
jaw	daidoli	lime	lumbor
job	vaazifa	linoleum	tarafaalu
joke	samaasa	light	ali
judo	gulamati hifang	lightening	vidaa
jump, to	fumani	lightweight	lui
jungle	valu	limestone	uva
		limp	koru
		line	rongu
kerosene	saaf teo	listen, to	adu ahani
key	talu dandi	little	kuda
kill, to	maraalani	live, to	uleni
kiss	dondeng	liver	me
kitchen	badige	lizard	bondu
kite	madi	loan	daranya
knee	kaku	lobster	ihi
knife	vali	lonely	fuhive
		long	digu
		look, to	balani
labourer	masekatu miha	loose	du
ladder	harugandu	loud	adugada
lamp	fulibati	love	lorbi
lantern	bigaru	low	tiri
large	bodu	lung	fupaame
late	las, lasvi	lucky	nasibu
laugh, to	heni		
lavatory	fahaana		
lawyer	vakeelu	mad	moia
lazy	kane	magic	jaadu
leaf	fai	maggot (worm)	fani
leak, to	diavani	make, to	hadani

176

mango – ripe	don ambu	narrow	hani
– green	hui ambu	nasty	nuba, gos
many	baivaru	nature	gudurat
map	chaatu	naughty	gos
marriage	kaveni	nautilus shell	fuenbari
mast	kumbu	neat	taahiru
mat	kunaa	near	kari
matches	alifang dandi	necklace	haaru
mate, to	jorduvani	needle	tinors
mattress	godadi	nest	haali
measure, to	minani	net	daa
medicine	bes	never	duahakves nuvaani
medium	medu	new	aa
meet, to	badalu kurani	news	habaru
melon	karaa	nice	riti
menstruate, to	hailuvani	noon	menduru
middle	medu, meduga	nose	nefai
midnight	mendang, medamu	not bad	nubā e nu
milk	kiru	not good	sākarai
mirror	lorgandu	nothing	eves eche nu
miscarriage	hiaru netung	nutmeg	takuva
mix, to	ekurani, modani	now	mihaaru
money	faisa		
monkey	raama makunu		
moon	handu		
more	ādi	oar	fali
morning	handunu	oath	huvaa
mortar	vang	obey, to	bas ahani
mosquito	madiri	occupation	maseka
mosquito coil	madiri dundandi	octopus	borva
mosquito net	madiri ge	odd	tafaatu
mountain	farubada	offensive	hadi
moustache	matimas	oil	teo
mouth	anga	okay	varihama
much	gina	old – people	muskuli
murder, to	maralani	– objects	baa
must	majuburu	omelette	bis gandu
mutton	bakari mas	onion	fia
		open	huluvifa
		open, to	huluvani
nail	morhoru	opinion	huvaa goi
naked	oriaanu	opium	afiung
name	nang, nama	or	nuvata, nuni

orange – colour	orenju	poison	viha
– fruit	foni lumbor	police	sifāng
out	beru	polish, to	ofu aruvani
outside	berufarai	pomegranate	anaaru
over	matiga	poor	fagiru
		pot	teli
		potato	aluvi
page	gandu, sorfa	– sweet	katela
painful	taduve	pound, to	talani
paint	davaadu	pork	uru mas
painting	mansaaru	prayer	duvaa
pair	jordu	present (gift)	hadia
palm	aitila	pretty	riti
paper	karudaas	pregnant	balive indefi
papaya	falor	previous	kurige
parcel	paasalu	price	agu
part	bā	problem	masala
passionate	lorbi	profit	fada
peanut	badang	prohibited	manaa
pearl	itaamvi	proud	foni
peel, to	mashani	pull, to	damani
peg – wooden	ili	pulse	vindu
– metal	kabila	pumpkin	barabor
pen	galang	punishment	adabu
pencil	fansuru	push, to	kopani
people	mihun	puss	dos
pepper	asemirus	put, to	bahaatani
perfect	baraabaru	putrid	kuni vefa
person	miha		
perspire, to	daahifuni		
pestle	mor	quantity	adadu
pig	uru	quarrel, to	araaruni
piece	etikolu	quay	faalang
pill	bes gula	queen – chess	mantiri
pillow	baalis	– cards	bibi
pimple	bihi	Queen	raani
pineapple	alanaasi	question	svaalu
pink	fiatoshi kula	quick	avaha, avas
place	tang	quiet	hamahimeng
place, to	bahaatani		
plane	matinda bortu		
plate	tashi	rabbit	musalu
pliers	kakuni	race, to	vaada jehani

rain	vaare, visaare	rub, to	ingulani
rain, to	vaare viheni	rubbish	kuni
rainbow	visaare duni	rudder	hungaanu
rainwater	vaare feng	ruler	fatigandu
raisin	mebiskaduru	run, to	duvani
rat	meeda	rust	dabaru
razor blade	rezaru tila		
read, to	kiani		
reason	sababu		
receipt	bilu		
recipe	kakan gvoi	sad	dera
red	rai kula	safe	rakaateri
reef	faru	sail	ria
refrigerator	ais alamaari	sail, to	duvani
relax, to	araam kurani	salad	sātani
remember, to	handaang kurani,	salary	musaara
	handaang hunani	salt	lornu
remove, to	nagani	sand	veli
rent	kuli	sandbank	finolhu
repair, to	hadani	sandpaper	hila karudaas
repeat, to	alung hadani	sarong	mundu
repent, to	towbaavani	say, to	bunani
reply	javabu	school	madurusā
rescue, to	salaame kurani	scissors	katuru
rest, to	varu bali riluvani	scrape, to	gaanani
reward	inaamu	scratch, to	kahani
rib	mekashi	screwpine	kashikeo
rice – cooked	bai	search, to	hordani
– raw	handu	season	musun
rich	musandi	secret	siru
ride, to	duvani	see, to	fenani
ridiculous	sākarai, gos	seed	or
ring	angorti	selfish	foni
rip, to	vidani	sell, to	vikani
ripe	don	send, to	fornuvani
roast, to	hanaa kurani	sentence	jumla
roof	furaalu	sew, to	fahani
room	kotari	shell	boli
rope	rornu	shirt	gamis
rotten	kunivefa	shoes	fāvang
rose	finifeng maa	shop	fihaara
round	vā	short	kuru
row, to	fali jehani	show, to	dakani
		shut, to	lapani

shadow	hiani	soup	suruva
shallow	tila	sour	hui
share, to	bahani	speak, to	vahaka dakani
shark	miaru	spear, to	hifani
sharp	tunu	spearfish	hibaru
short	kuru	spectacles	ainu
shy	ladu	spicy	kuli
sick	balive	spider	fādigu makunu
side	farai	spit, to	kulu jehani
sideburns	kanghuli	spoilt	gosvefa
sign, to	soi kurani	spoon	samsaa
signature	soi	square	hatareskang
silly	seku	stand, to	teduvani
silver	rihi	star	tari
similar	egvoy	start, to	fashani
simple	faseha	stay, to	hunani
sin	faafa	steal, to	vakani
sing, to	lava kiani	stingray	madi
sit, to	ishinani	stomach	bandu
skin	hang	stone	hila
sky	udu	stop, to	madu kurani
slave	alu	storeroom	bandaha ge
sleep, to	nidani	storm	kuli gandu
slow	las, lasvi	story	vahaka
small	kuda	stove	undung
smart-arse	foni miha	straight	tedu
smile, to	hununi	strike, to	jahani
smooth	ormang	string	vaa kole
smell	vas	strong	varugada
smoke	dung	studious	ilmuvering
smoke, to	borni	stupid	seku
snake	harufa	succeed	kaamiaabu
sneeze, to	kimbihi alani	sugar	hakuru
soap	sāborni	suicide, to	amilaa maruvani
socks	istaakinu	sun	iru
soft	madu	sunshade	hiaa
some	bai, eketikolu	sure	gamu
something	komes eche	swallow, to	diruvaalani
song	lava	sweet	foni
sore	tadu	sweet potato	katela
sorry	maaf kure	swim, to	fatani
sort, to	horvani	swing, to	helani
sound	adu	swordfish	hibaru

table	mezu	time	vagatu, gadi
tablet	gula	tin	dalu
tack, to (sailing)	ambrani	to	a
tailor	fahaa miha	toast	rorst paan
take, to	nagani	tobacco	dung fai
tall	digu	today	miadu
tank	taangi	toe	ingili
taro	ala	together	ekuga
taste	raha	tomato	vilaatu bashi
tasty	vara miru	tomorrow	maadama
tea – leaves	säfai	tongue	du
– cup of	sä	tonight	mire
– cup	jordu	tooth	dai
– pot	säkuraa	toothache	datuga rihung
– strainer	säfurene	toothpaste	dai ungula bes
telescope	duruming	touch, to	ai laani
tell, to	bunani	towel	tuvaali
temperature	hunuming	translator	tarujamaaru miha
terrific	baraabaru	tray	dolangu
that	e	tree	gas
thatch	fang	trial	sarie
therefore	ehenvimaa	triangle	tinkang
these	mi	trousers	fatulung
thick	fala	true	tedu
thief	vagu miha	trust	itubaaru
thigh	fala mas gandu	tumeric	rindu
thin – people	hiki	tuna	kandumas
– objects	hani	turtle	velaa, kahambu
think, to	visnani	twins	e maabundu
thing	eche	two-faced	defu keheri
this	mi		
thongs	fävang		
those	e		
thread	rodi	ugly	huturu
throat	karu	umbrella	kudta
through	tereng	unavailable	libeka ne
throw, to	elani	under	dashuga
thunder	gugurung	underground	bimu adi
tide	diavaru	undress, to	hedung baalani
tidy	taahiru	unfinished	nunime
tight	baaru	unhappy	deravefa
tiller	hungaanu	unlock, to	tandu natani
timber	la kudi	unlucky	badu nasibu

unmarried	husariba	well – hole	valu
unravel, to	niulani	– health	gada
unripe	giti	wet	te
untidy	hadi	what	korche
upper	mati	wheat	godang
use, to	benung kurani	wheel	frolu
		when	kong ira kung
		where	kong taka
vacant	husvefa	which	kong
valet	banderi	white – colour	hudu
vegetables	tarukari	– skin	don
veins	naaru	who	kaaku
very	vara	whose	kaakuge
vicious	jaahilu	why	kivi
vinegar	raahui	wide	fulaa
voice	adu	wind	va
vomit, to	hordulani	window	kuda doru
vowel	fili	wipe, to	forheni
voyage	daturu	wire	naru
		wise	budi gada
		wish, to	eduni
wage	musaara	with	eku, ekuga
waist	una gandu	without	nula
waste	kuni	witness	heking miha
wait, to	madu kurani	wok	taas
walk, to	hingani	wooden spoon	unduli, defai
wall	faaru	wool	keheri
want, to	benumi	world	dunie
war	hanguraama	work	masekai
wash, to	donani	write, to	liani
watch, to	balani		
water – rain	vaare feng		
– well	valu feng	yellow	rindu kula
watermelon	karaa	young – people	zuvaang
waves	raalu	– objects	la
wax	u		
weak – objects	bali		
– people	varu dera	zoo	haivaanu bagicha
weapon	hatiaaru	zuchini	tora
weather	musun		
weave, to	vihani		
wedding	kaveni sā		
weight	baruming		

182

Suggested readings

Adeney, M. and Carr, W. K., "The Maldives Republic", *The Politics of the Western Indian Ocean Islands*, London, Praeger Publishers.

Agassiz, A., "The Coral Reefs of the Maldives", *Memoirs of the Museum of Comparative Zoology at Harvard College*, Vol XXLX, USA, Cambridge University Press, 1903 — a topographical survey of the Maldivian atolls.

Baksi-Lahiri, Sudeshna, *Women's Power and Ritual Politics in the Maldives*, (unpublished), Fulbright-Hays Doctoral Dissertation Program, 1981 — an academic's view of the woman's role in Maldivian society.

Battuta, Ibn, *Ibn Battuta in the Maldives and Ceylon*, edited by Albert Gray, Colombo, Royal Asiatic Society, 1881 — memoirs of a 14th century traveller.

Bell, H.C.P., *The Maldive Islands: An Account of the Physical Features, Climate, History, Inhabitants, Production and Trade*, Colombo, Government Printer, 1883.
and
Report on a Visit to Male, Colombo, Government Printer, 1920
and
The Maldive Islands: Monograph on the History, Archaeology and Epigraphy, Colombo, Government Printer, 1940 — the most important journals on Maldivian history.

Bowder, Jim, *Maldive Islands Money*, California, Society for International Numismatics, 1969 — a look at ancient Maldivian currency.

Butany, W.T., *Report on Agricultural Survey and Crop Production*, Rome, UNDP, 1974 — a review of the major Maldivian crops and agricultural problems.

Colton, Elizabeth, *Maldives Looks to the Future*, Hong Kong, Far Eastern Economic Review, October 1979 — an interview with the President of the Maldives.

Crowe, Philip K., *Diversions of a Diplomat in Ceylon*, London, Macmillan and Co., 1957 — a short chapter on life in Male by a former British ambassador to Ceylon.

de Silva, M.W.S., *Some Observations on the History of the Maldivian language*, Oxford, The Philological Society, 1970.

Didi, M.A., *Ladies and Gentlemen — The Maldive Islands*, Male, Ministry of External Affairs, 1949 — an account by a former President of the Maldives.

Forbes, Andrew D.W., "Weaving in the Maldive Islands", *Occasional Paper No. 9*, London, British Museum — a look at the mat industry in Suvadive atoll.
    and
Southern Arabia and the Islamicisation of the Central Indian Ocean Archipelagoes, Paris, Archipel 21, 1981 — an account of how Islam spread to the Maldives.
    and
Archives and Resources for Maldivian History, Sudan, University of Khartoum — a review of the best literature on Maldivian history.

Gardiner, Stanley J., *The Fauna and Geography of the Maldive Islands*, USA, Cambridge University Press, 1906.

Gupta, Ranjan, *The Indian Ocean*, Bombay, Marwah Publications — a short chapter on the geopolitics of the Maldives.

Hass, Hans "Central Subsistence: A new theory of atoll formation", *Atoll Research Bulletin*, Washington D.C., Pacific Science Board, 1962 — a possible alternative to Darwin's theory.

Health, Ministry of, *On the way toward health for all*, Vol 1, Male, UNICEF, 1980 — a program of health statistics.

Hockly, T.W., *The Two Thousand Isles*, London, H.F. & G. Witherby, 1935 — an account of the people, history, and customs of the Maldives.

Information, Department of, *The Maldive Islands Today*, Male, — a brief look at some facets of society by various local authors.

Innes, Hammond, *Sea and Islands*, London, Collins, 1967 — a novel whose theme is set around the southern Maldivian atolls.

Kurian, George Thomas, *Encyclopaedia of the Third World*, Vol. 2, London, Mansell, 1979 — a basic fact sheet.

Lateef, K., *An Introductory Economic Report*, Washington D.C., The World Bank, 1980 — a documentary on the Maldivian economy.

Maloney Clarence, "The Maldives: New Stresses in an Old Nation", *Asian Survey*, California, University of California Press, 1976
and
People of the Maldive Islands, New Delhi, Orient Longman, 1980 — a sociological dissection of the Maldivian people.

Maniku, Hassan, *The Maldives — a profile*, Male, Department of Information, 1977.
and
The Republic of Maldives — some facts, Male, Universal Enterprises, 1980
and
The History of the Maldivian Constitution, (unpublished), Male, Department of Information, 1982 — some of the books by today's most renowned Maldivian author.

Moresby, Robert, *Nautical Directions for the Maldive Islands*, London, Allen & Co., 1840.

Mukerjee, Dilip, *Maldives Diversifies Contacts with Big Neighbours*, London, Pacific Community, 1975 — a look at "big troubles Thursday".

Munch-Peterson, N.F., *Background Paper for Population Needs Mission*, Rome, UNDP, 1981 — a brief resume on Maldivian society

Phadnis, Urmila and Luithui, Ela Dutt, "The Maldives Enter World Politics", *Asian Affairs*, January 1981.

Pyrard, Francois, *The Voyages of Francois Pyrard of Laval to the East Indies, the Maldives, the Moluccas and Brazil*, Vol. 1, London, Hakluyt Society, 1887 — a detailed account of the 17th century Maldivian customs.

Reynolds, C.H.B., *The Maldive Islands*, London, Royal Central Asian Society, 1974.
and

Linguistic Strands in the Maldives, London, School of Oriental and Asian Studies, 1978.

Rosset, C.W., *The Maldive Islands*, London, The Graphic, October 1886 — impressions of Male by a 19th century visitor.

Seidler, Helen, *Report on the Survey of Island Women*, Male, National Planning Agency, 1980 — a statistical overview of a woman's role in Maldivian society.

Smallwood, C., *A Visit to the Maldive islands*, London, Royal Central Asian Society, 1961 — a review of the Maldvies by a former captain of the British Air Force.

Stoddard, T.L., *Area Handbook for the Indian Ocean Territories*, Washington D.C., American University, 1971.

Villiers, Alan, *Give Me a Ship to Sail*, London, Hodden & Stoughton, 1958.
and
The Marvellous Maldive Islands, Washington D.C., National Geographic Society, June 1957 — impressions of Male and its inhabitants by a renowned author and sailor.

Young, I.A. and Christopher W., *Memoir on the Inhabitants of the Maldive Islands*, Bombay, Bombay Geographical Society, 1844 — important memoirs by two 19th century naval officers.

Photo credits

Index

Distributors

Australia

Other People ,
27 Segers Avenue,
Padstow, NSW. 2211.

Singapore and
Malaysia

MPH Bookstores (S) Pte. Ltd.,
PAN-1 Warehouse Complex,
3rd Storey, 601 Sims Drive,
#03-21, Singapore 1438.

Sri Lanka

Jeya Agency,
54 Ratnakara Place,
Dehiwela.

United Kingdom

Roger Lascelles,
47 York Road,
Brentford,
Middlesex. TW8 OQP.